Managers as strategists

D1471722

Managers as strategists

Health services managers reflecting on practice

Edited by Greg Parston

King Edward's Hospital Fund for London

Printed and bound in England by Hollen Street Press Ltd

King's Fund Publishing Office
2 St Andrew's Place
London NW1 4LB

Contents

List of contributors

Gordon Best	Director, King's Fund College
R W Dearden	Chief Executive, National Health Services Training Authority
Tom Evans	Director, King's Fund College until his death in 1985
David King	District General Manager, Exeter Health Authority
Richard M Knapp	Director, Department of Teaching Hospitals, Association of American Medical Colleges
Stephen R Leeder	Professor of Community and Geriatric Medicine, University of Sydney
A S Macpherson	Medical Officer of Health, Department of Public Health, Toronto
Duncan K Nichol	Regional General Manager, Mersey Regional Health Authority
Richard A Norling	President, California Medical Center, Los Angeles
Greg Parston	Fellow and Coordinator of Field Development Programmes, King's Fund College
Andrew M Pettigrew	Director, Centre for Corporate Strategy and Change, University of Warwick
George Salmond	Director-General, Department of Health, New Zealand
Leonard D Schaeffer	President, Blue Cross of California

Introduction

Managers learn from thinking critically about their own work. By assessing their own experience and performance, managers learn more about the phenomena that face them and their organisations; they gain a greater appreciation of their own behaviour as managers. By reflecting on their own practice, managers become better practitioners and learn how to deal more successfully with the uncertainty and the complexity that are their daily realities.

In his enlightening study of how professionals learn while doing, *The Reflective Practitioner*, Donald Schön points out that although managers do reflect on their actions, they seldom reflect on that reflection. They seldom articulate what they have learned. 'Hence this crucially important dimension of their art tends to remain private and inaccessible to others', resulting amongst other things in the 'mysteriousness of the art of managing' and a weakening of the manager's ability to help others learn.[1]

This book is a contribution to managers' helping each other to learn. Most of the papers in the book are written by health services managers; they are not someone else's account of what those managers do or say they do, but the thoughts of the managers themselves on their own work, and on their relative successes and failures. The book is a collection of papers which were first written for discussion during an international seminar on Managers as Strategists, sponsored by the King's Fund with support from the Kellogg Foundation, and held in Canberra, Australia, in October 1985. The seminar included twenty-four outstanding health care managers and policy-makers from the United Kingdom, the United States, Canada, Australia, and New Zealand. Together, they spent a week trying to come to grips with the difficult notion of managing strategy, not as an abstract concept but as the application of their own efforts to the problems and opportunities which they confront as managers. After the seminar, several of the participants' papers were revised to reflect the co-learning that had taken place and those papers are included here. A complete list of all of the seminar participants is included at the end of this book.

Managers as strategists

A manager's strategy depends upon a number of things, perhaps most importantly upon the environment of the manager's organisation – both inner and outer. The inner environment comprises people, systems, structures and their melding together into behavioural patterns that are fashionably referred to as organisational culture. The outer environment is made up of all the uncontrollable, often unknowable, uncertainties and complexities that can influence and sometimes determine the trajectory of the organisation. A manager's strategy is formed in an effort to negotiate the boundaries between these inner and outer environments. But because the inner environment can be more or less cohesive and the outer environment can be more or less turbulent, and because both are likely to be changing at any time, strategies vary between organisations and over time. By the same argument, strategy for any one organisation at any one time is unique.

The diversity and uniqueness of strategy can make problematic any group discussions amongst managers of what a strategy is, of how it is formed, and of what role it has in the management of an organisation. Each manager's view is made different by their diverse and unique circumstances. As a result, common understandings can be difficult to achieve, agreements may be unreachable, and the value of the discussions themselves may be questionable. In many ways, the very idea of strategy can plague a seminar on managers as strategists. And, to some extent, that happened in the case of the Canberra conference, largely because of the great variations in the phenomena which managers from the representative countries encounter in their own work.

While there is an increasing emphasis on management performance in the health systems of each of the countries represented at the seminar, there are marked differences in the levels and directions of the environmental changes buffeting their respective health care organisations and managers. The largely private, heavily-entrepreneurial, market forces of the US health care industry, for example, stand in stark contrast to the highly-politicised, public sector manipulations of the British National Health Service. The result is that while the vocabularies of health managers in the two countries have their similarities, their languages are not the same. Similarly, while Canadian, Australian and New Zealand managers are equally glib with phrases such as 'clinical accountability', 'effectiveness and efficiency' and 'environmental turbulence', the national and financial contexts of the organisational changes they are charged with implementing can lend those words remarkably different connotations.

During the seminar, these differences were most apparent in what seemed at first an undercurrent of disagreement about the nature of strategy. This eventually surfaced, however, as a lengthy debate, not about strategy at all, but about the role of the manager in the public sector. The opposing arguments tended to set the Americans, many of whom saw their roles as entrepeneurs in a market where only the fittest survive, against the British, some of whom appeared more concerned about developing their organisations' future capabilities than about questions of immediate survival. Managers of the other countries joined in the argument, but where individual managers stood in the end had little to do with nationality and more to do with the public or private ownership of their organisations. At the heart of the debate was a view that managers in the public sector have comparatively little worry about where their revenues are coming from. Because of this, several of the private sector managers characterised their public-sector counterparts as 'more administrator than manager', carrying out budgetary decisions made by others in central government, and not having to worry in the same way about developing strategies that withstand financial uncertainties. Of course, public sector managers disagreed.

Compounding the conflict were the recent experiences of the British managers – all of whom had been made chief executives as a result of a 1984 NHS reorganisation that did away with consensus management teams and introduced the position of general manager. While admitting that income–generation was not as high a priority on their agenda, those in the public sector regarded the need to maximise service provision in conditions of great political uncertainty as a responsibility as daunting as any of those of their private sector colleagues. They argued that in some respects, as for example in the bureaucratic restrictions placed on their abilities to respond rapidly to change, public sector managers may face even a more difficult job. Clearly some public sector health organisations provide more effective and efficient services than others and part of the reason for this, it was argued, is better management in diagnosing problems, in identifying and exploiting opportunities, in strengthening organisational capabilities, and in developing strategies – tasks and processes not dissimilar to those of the private sector manager.

These differences were never satisfactorily resolved and, indeed, the informal debate amongst the managers participating in the international seminar still rages. But participants struggled through their conceptual and semantic differences to find shared meaning and common ground. They were aided by papers, prepared by faculty of the seminar, which attempted to move discussion toward a more general understanding of strategic management and of managers as strategists. These papers are included here as well. Among them, the paper by Tom Evans, 'Strategic Response to Environmental Turbulence', served as the theme paper of the seminar, relating the concepts of strategy, organisational capability and learning to management in both the private and the public sector. Tom's tragic death months before the International Seminar deprived these managers of the insight and thinking that undoubtedly would have made their joint deliberations even more fruitful.

By the end of the seminar, several clear ideas emerged. They include the inter-relationship between strategy and organisational capability; the cycle of diagnosis, development, stability and learning; the dynamics of content, context and process in the management of change; the importance of the interplay between management task and managerial process; and the recognition that organisations can have many different strategies whose orchestration is the role of the strategic manager. These ideas come up time and again in this book. There is no need to rehearse them here, but it might be useful to cite the observations of Philip Berman, Director of the European Association of Programmes in Health Services Studies, regarding the qualities that participants learned are required of their own behaviour if they are to succeed as strategic managers:

A mixture of sensitivity and toughness – the former to be able to gauge both the external and internal environments and to assess the risks of the failure, and the latter to persist with the strategies selected and to ensure that the organisation is moving in a purposeful direction.

The wisdom to refrain from managing the components of the organisation but rather to provide leadership in two principal areas: interpreting the environment to the organisation and the organisation to the environment, and managing the interplay between tasks and processes when change is required.

The skill to spot both the leading edge of an activity – the opportunity for the organisation – and its peak and decline, so that the organisation can engage and disengage to maximum advantage. In effect this means recognising life-cycles in the way that any fashion industry has had to do.

A commitment to the importance of organisational learning, being able to demonstrate how he or she can create success out of crisis or failure. Leaders must provide the environment, motivation and vision for learning. They must also build the internal capability to cope with continuing uncertainty and unforeseen situations.[2]

Structure of the book

The papers in this book are grouped into four sections, each related to one of the sub-themes that had been identified by Tom Evans and Robert Maxwell in planning the Managers as Strategists seminar. These were: environmental assessment; strategic planning – the process; strategic approaches to management of change; and the development strategy. Each section begins with a faculty member's paper which explores issues related to the sub-theme. During the sessions of the seminar, these papers provided general frameworks within which the participant managers considered their own experiences and from which they tried to draw out general principles and lessons. Papers written by the managers similarly concentrated on particular sub-themes and these follow in each section. Because these papers had been read beforehand, they provided common case studies for group assessment and critique during each session, but they also prompted other managers to make associations between the reflections in their own papers and their own work and the overlapping sub-themes.

Like the seminar's sub-themes, the sections are not conceptually separable or self-contained, nor are the management actions on which they focus. Assessing the environment, planning strategy, managing change, and developing organisational capabilities are overlapping, interdependent and simultaneous activities of the strategic manager. So, in one paper, a manager focuses on how the popular desires in the local environment are influencing the direction of his health authority, but we also see the initial formations of the organisation's response to those influences and the processes by which necessary changes are being shaped. Another manager's concerns for organisational performance and development in his medical school are related directly to an assessment of a tension in the outer environment between the inadequacy of traditional approaches to medical education and the public's strongly-held expectations of doctors' roles. And yet another manager considers how the establishment of a new strategic planning approach has provided an opportunity and a focus for organisational and management development.

Many of the papers highlight personal achievements, several of them raise risks of potential failure. They each try to identify what the manager has learned, often by identifying some major tasks and changes that lie ahead. But there is no advocacy of a standardised formula for success. There is no suggestion of a performance checklist for the strategic manager. What this collection of papers tries most to do is to use these managers' reflections to encourage other managers to look critically into their own work and to see in it a source for their own learning.

References

1 Schön, Donald. The Reflective Practitioner: How Professionals Think in Action. London, Temple Smith, 1983: p 243.
2 Berman, Philip. 'Managers as Strategists: A Report of an International Seminar', Hospital and Health Services Review, November 1986.

Managing the environment

Introduction

The first paper in this book is 'Strategic Response to Environmental Turbulence' by Tom Evans, who was Director of the King's Fund College. This was a working paper that was given to seminar participants to introduce them to the theme of Managers as Strategists. The paper was incomplete, a thoughts-in-progress piece, meant to be redrafted after the seminar discussions. Unfortunately, Tom was unable to complete the paper before his death. Although some of his colleagues have now redrafted the paper for future publication, it is reproduced here unedited and in its original draft form. It is that version of the paper which prompted the seminar participants' own thinking about strategic management and thus it influenced many of the other papers which are included in this book.

Tom Evans' paper is not only about environmental assessment – the opening theme of the seminar – but more broadly about managing in the face of uncertainty, complexity, and change. By trying to draw lessons from private sector management and considering them within the different but no less turbulent environment of the public sector, the paper foreshadowed some of the debate that emerged in the seminar. The paper begins by exploring the relationships between environmental turbulence, strategy, and planning as they have evolved in private sector business organisations. The growth of discontinuity and surprise and the increasing complexity of the environment are cited, amongst other factors, as having contributed to a loss of confidence in conventional approaches to environmental assessment, forecasting and planning. This in turn has placed greater emphasis on developing an organisation's abilities to cope with uncertainty and change and to learn while doing so.

The lessons that have been gained in the private sector also include a recognition of strategy as a means to guide and control organisational process and an increased reliance on analysis to support rather than replace managerial judgement and debate. Evans considers the applicability of these lessons with respect to organisations in the public sector, where constraints on managerial actions and the frequent lack of sanctions are sometimes cited as causes for pessimism amongst public sector managers. He dismisses this pessimism and argues that the public sector, too, requires a new view of strategy to deal with its own brands of turbulence and limitations. The paper ends by introducing a conceptual framework for strategic management that links an organisation's substantive activities to its capabilities, that integrates organisational diagnosis and development, and that emphasises the needs for continuous analysis and for organisational learning.

This theme paper explores the dynamic interplay between organisational behaviour and environmental uncertainty, and in doing so it stresses the need for continuing assessment of factors in the environment which challenge the strategic manager. In another briefing paper prepared before the seminar to stimulate participants' thinking and writing about specific sub-themes, three levels of environmental assessment had been identified: first is a scan of national, regional and local factors; second, a consideration of activities and trends within the industry; and third, an examination of the implications of these external environmental factors upon the organisation. The papers in this section that are written by health service managers demonstrate the importance of all three levels of environmental assessment.

George Salmond's case study of how the needs of the Maori people of New Zealand are beginning to be reflected in the health policies of that country underscores how important it is for managers to be constantly aware of, and sensitive to, the environment's global influences. The Maoris' needs include those of personal health care, but they also have to do with cultural integrity, with social practices and with community politics. Ignoring any one of these concerns can result in poor local health service provision but, worse, it can disrupt unconsciously other national developments in a resurging people.

In the United States, an increasingly competitive economic climate is making the price of health care a principal consideration in managerial and organisational decision-making. While many in the US health industry regard the overall effects of these developments as largely positive, there are adverse side-effects. Richard Knapp's paper considers how the shared costs of medical care and medical education are affected by price-competitiveness and concludes that the ultimate result might be a medical service system which nobody wants. His assessment of activities and trends in the health industry raises important issues for its managers; more generally, it demonstrates the importance of continuous analysis of the variance between expectation and outcome.

David King's paper demonstrates the influences of environmental factors not only on organisational process and behaviour, but also on the manager's own values. The strong desire among people living in his health authority for small local services posed a fundamental challenge to the philosophy of centralism which had dominated his thinking as a British NHS manager. In this case study, the development of strategy is actually a negotiation with the environment, learning more about what the people want, and reshaping the organisation to be able to respond purposefully. King concludes by reflecting upon how far he has had to shift his own attitudes in order to manage these transitions in a demanding environment.

One point which emerges from the sequence of these managers' papers is the interrelationships between the various levels of environmental turbulence. The patterns of services that are demanded locally can be encouraged and obstructed simultaneously by activities at national and regional levels; at the same time, emerging national trends can unintendedly and adversely affect an industry's overall ability to react opportunistically to local needs. A manager's response may have to be to incorporate local pressures directly into the organisation's processes of change; yet what may seem a correct response at one level may jeopardise success at others. Managers must have a clear understanding and a sensitive appreciation of these interrelationships and of their impacts on organisational performance and action. Without that, formulating a strategic response to a turbulent environment would be doubtful.

1

Strategic response to environmental turbulence

TOM EVANS

Introduction

The idea that the environment in which modern organisations work is more complex, demanding and unpredictable than it once was has dominated the literature of corporate planning and strategy over the last 20 years. Though the year 1973 and the OPEC crisis underlined the growing incapacity of planning practice to cope with environmental change, many of the ideas had been stated earlier in what are now classic texts.[1,2] Common to the extensive literature that has followed is the notion that the texture of the environment is changing in a way which outstrips the capacity of traditional methods of prediction, analysis and adaptation, and which consequently requires the development of new and greater organisational capabilities. At this point a clear and profound schism appears. There is a rational orthodoxy, which believes that a marked improvement in analytical competence is required, but that this is consistent with the assumptions and perspectives of existing paradigms. The alternative looks for a revolution in mind, seeking to define a radically different paradigm and hence a different focus for corporate strategy and planning. The schism is ever-present in the modern literature and in contemporary debates about strategy and planning, though the assumptions and implicit values of the position being adopted are not always explicitly recognised in practice.[3] In the interests of fair interpretation and of the application of the reader's scepticism, I should make clear at the outset that this essay is written from a basis which is closer to the second perspective. Consequently, the argument of this paper depends upon an explanation of the concepts and assumptions which characterise this perspective and a display of the practical issues which arise from it.

The term 'turbulence' has crept into the language as an immediately recognisable description of a discomforting, unsettling state of the world, of which we all have experience. Yet the original use of the term by Emery and Trist[4] involved a discriminating classification of four states of an organisational environment and an analysis both of the characteristics of type 4 (turbulent) environments and of the challenges they pose for organisational effectiveness and success. These characteristics are described in terms of the interconnectedness of elements in the environment and their propensity to be dynamically 'self-exciting'. That is to say, environmental uncertainties arise and are simplified not merely as a consequence of the organisation's own action. Emery and Trist describe the phenomenon and the appropriate strategies of response as:

> ' ... the dynamic properties arise not simply from the interaction of the component organisations, but also from the field itself. The 'ground' is in motion ... For organisations, these trends mean a gross increase in their area of *relevant uncertainty*. The consequences which flow from their actions lead off in ways that become increasingly unpredictable; they do not necessarily fall off with distance, but may at any point be amplified beyond all expectation; similarly lines of action that are strongly pursued may find themselves attenuated by emergent field forces ... In these environments individual organisations, however large, cannot expect to adapt successfully through their own direct actions ... the solution lies in the emergence of *values that have overriding significance for all members of the field* ... turbulent environments require some relationship between dissimilar organisations where fates are basically, positively correlated.'[5]

While neither the full flavour of this concept of turbulence nor the diagnosis of appropriate responses have necessarily been replicated in the subsequent literature, the two most important characteristics of the idea are already clear here, namely:

> that environmental uncertainty is not merely induced by an organisation's actions and that it may not be resolvable solely through that organisation's own strategy;

> that a quantum leap from traditional organisational responses is required, not merely a refinement or extension of them. In Emery and Trist's case, this is the shift from competitive to cooperative strategies for dealing with the environment.

These two themes recur in the literature, even though the concept of environmental turbulence used is often less specific and refined.

In this essay I shall explore these issues of environmental turbulence, corporate strategy and planning in two stages. First, I shall consider the concepts as they have been employed in the private business world. Even there we can detect a substantial evolution in the concepts of strategy and planning in response to what are perceived as turbulent environments. In the practice of strategy and planning, this evolution often surfaces as dilemmas and questions rather than as any radical shift of method. In the second part, I apply the ideas of turbulence, strategy and planning to public services which are not market based, to show that these conditions emphasise precisely the qualities which we had identified in emerging strategic concepts in the private sector.

Strategic management and planning

THE CONCEPT OF STRATEGY

The concept of strategy as identifying the common thread of an organsiation's activity is now commonplace. So, for example, Andrews gives a representative view of corporate strategy as:

> 'the pattern of major objectives, purposes, or goals and essential policies and plans for achieving those goals, stated in such a way as to define what business the company is in or is to be in and the kind of company it is or is to be. In a changing world it is a way of expressing a persistent concept of the business so as to exclude some possible new activities and suggest entry into others.'[6]

Such a view emphasises the importance for, say, a manufacturing company of finding some themes in developing its products and the market areas in which it will choose to compete. The private market-oriented firm is able to make substantial changes over a period of time in its markets, its products, and its methods of competition. Not surprisingly the concept of strategy which emerged emphasised such changes as a means of dealing with uncertainties (and opportunities) in its environment, and saw strategy as a means of plotting a coherent and purposive path through the many options of market and product adjustment open to the firms. So, one of the classic writers on corporate strategy, Igor Ansofff[7], identified four components of strategy:

1 Product market scope: the industrial areas to which the firm limits its activities, or indeed whether it does limit itself in this way.

2 Growth vector: what means does the firm use to seek growth? For example, further penetration of existing markets, developing

new products, developing new markets for existing products, diversification into new product market areas.

3 Competitive advantage: what is the basis of the firm's competitive advantage in its present or new markets; for example, cost, product quality, patent protection?

4 Synergy: how far are any new developments aided by the firm's existing expertise, technology, manufacturing facilities, or market position?

The intention is to find opportunities which the company has an advantage in exploiting because of its identified strengths. Or, to put it another way, the company seeks to adjust its linkages to the environment (products, markets, and so on) to produce the greatest congruence with its competitive strengths. Strategy is the representation of how this matching is seen at any point in time. The primary focus is on adjustment through changing the linkages into the environment rather than the internal capability of the organisation.

Out of an analysis of these factors a firm can derive both a sense of direction in its search for opportunity and criteria by which to judge any proposed option. Such is the function of strategy. Much of the work that was built on these foundations concerned the development of an analytical framework with which to define corporate strategies in practice.

To understand why these basic concepts of strategy have run into difficulty in practice, especially in the face of complex and turbulent environments, we must consider briefly the role of planning in sustaining the development of strategy and, in particular, problems in forecasting, in strategic analysis and in the process of defining and using corporate strategy.

PLANNING AND STRATEGY

In the vintage of planning which was contemporaneous with these concepts of strategy, strategic planning was seen as forecasting environmental change (and hence reducing the uncertainty facing the organisation), and developing a coherent strategy through the analysis of options.

In its most naive versions, prediction of the future seeks to buffer decision-makers within the organisation from the vagaries of the environment by providing them with an assumption of what it will be like. Whether this is in the form of a 'point' forecast – 'GDP will grow at 3.2 per cent' – or an 'interval' forecast – 'there is a 60 per cent chance that GDP will grow between 3.0 per cent and 3.4 per cent' – the intent is to provide a reliable assumption upon which decisions can be based. However, a number of factors have served to reduce confidence in the predictability of environmental change and hence of this role for forecasting:

The growth of discontinuity and surprise in the environment Some writers, particularly Ansoff in his later writings[8], have argued that the major characteristic of the environment is the growing incidence of discontinuity and surprise. It is not always clear precisely what this means but, first, it may refer to events in which something happens that is by definition not a continuous variation of its not happening. So 'war' and 'no war' are discrete, discontinuous events. Second, there may be threshold effects in behaviour, as when continuous variation in inputs produces sudden change in output behaviour. Finally, the underlying pattern of relationships of input to output behaviour may suddenly change. It is conceptually very difficult to distinguish these three types of change but, in principle at least, they pose different problems for forecasting. It may be argued that many events are threshold effects, but others surely are the result of go/no-go decisions by major actors. The latter may include election outcomes or the subsequent political decisions of the elected government.

Increasing complexity As relationships between variables in the organisation's environment become more intricate, two major consequences follow. First, a wider range of factors has to be regarded as relevant to the company. Second it becomes more difficult to trace and model the structure of relationships between factors. Clearly, forecasting then has to take into account future values of a wider range of variables and depends on modelling more extensive structures. For example, there is widespread recognition of the growing relative importance of socio-political variables compared with economic factors in determining the future conditions facing companies. Forecasting socio-political factors requires a different technical approach and data sources.[9,10]

Quality of data input As the range of factors included in forecasting is extended, it is difficult to maintain the quality of data sources which might be possible in a narrower and more well-tried domain. In particular, the more forecasting is driven to use data not derived from a company's own activities or market areas, the more is it dependent on ad hoc information or data produced by others for quite different purposes. It then becomes more difficult to guarantee the quality of the data, or even to estimate reliably how good or bad it is.

These are very orthodox and well-established suspicions about the emergent difficulties of forecasting, but they drive us to consider the role of forecasting if its reliability or quality is suspect.

The development of methods which provide a means of exploring the future rather than producing a specific prediction have become increasingly familiar. Methods of combining judgments as to future development (Delphi), or of tracing the interrelationship of future events (cross-impact matrices), or of analysing alternative configurations of future characteristics (scenarios) are now commonplace. But the important general issue is the adaptation of methods of prediction to the ways in which anticipation of the future is being used.

For instance, forecasting may be given responsibility as a general scanning device to search for and define changes in the environment which threaten or create opportunity for the organisation. In this role, forecasting would be involved in creating an agenda for concern and action within the company. Or, in relation to the longer term, forecasting may perform functions of what Cole calls 'informative speculation'[11] and may address itself to developing awareness or understanding of options. Whatever the specifics, the conventional assumptions about the role and practice of forecasting undoubtedly come under stress from more intractable or more complex environments. One facet of a concept of strategy for turbulent environments would be an approach to structuring uncertainty that goes beyond forecasting and stresses ways of coping with remaining uncertainties, rather than purporting to remove them through prediction.

Similar problems have appeared in the analysis of strategic options, though they need not detain us here. Corporate strategic analysis is concerned largely with the portfolio of products the company has or is developing, with the markets to which it has access, and the basis of its competitiveness in existing and potential markets. What is important is how this portfolio hangs together now and in the future. Not surprisingly, the analytical methods which have been developed reflect the need to examine the qualities of the portfolio, usually by defining cells of a matrix and plotting the distribution of activities across them. For instance, the Boston Consulting Group (BCG) method[12] defines a 2 x 2 matrix identifying different levels of market share against different rates of market growth. Or the more complex Directional Policy Matrix[13] identifies a 3 x 3 matrix, taking as its dimensions the company's competitive capabilities and the prospects for sector profitability. Wensley[14] offers a number of criticisms of these methods which show up the difficulties of strategic analysis, particularly in poorly structured or complex environments. From him we may learn some lessons about the limitations of analysis that seeks to generate relatively simple prescriptive rules.

First, these methods are made obscure by using proxy variables for underlying, and more relevant, conditions. So, market share stands as an indicator of relative competitiveness in BCG, because it is backed by the presumption of an associated cost advantage based on an experience curve. Or again, BCG assumes the superiority of investment in high growth areas. This assumption should sometimes be amended by reference to the company's relative competitive skills and the competitors' response. If everybody invests in high growth areas, what competitive advantage does the firm have? If everybody is quitting low growth areas, are there not possibilities for competitive gain there?

Second, Wensley suggests that such methods are less than explicit about the real strategic criteria involved. For instance, if matrix methods suggest preferred investment in high growth areas, is it suggested that projects in such areas should be accepted, even if their present value on a discounted cash flow (DCF) calculation is low, simply because they are in high growth areas? In other words, is there a strategic criterion which should be followed even though it contradicts the DCF assessment? If the answere is no, then the approach is merely a prediction that projects in high growth areas will yield high present values, and adds nothing to DCF analysis. If the answer is yes, then what is the nature and justification of this strategic cri terion whose worth does not show up in the DCF assessment? The exploration of these indirect benefits is not well exposed by global (and empirically unsubstantiated) assumptions about the values of being in growing markets. It requires a more detailed and system atic assessment of competitive advantage. So, for instance, the impact of a project on barriers to entry, or barriers to mobility[15], or in creating locational advantages which are options to undertake further profitable investment, might represent a strategic criterion of some value, but these effects would need to be analysed explicitly.

In a very important sense, these are not arguments against portfolio or matrix analysis, but rather against their mechanistic application. As diagnostic tools in skilled hands, they have been powerful. But the superficial gloss of analysis has equally often proved misleading if it is not filtered through the judgments of good managers. Once again, we have had to learn painfully the limitations of analysis in order to appreciate its real benefits as an aid.

What emerges is a picture in which the basis of strategic thinking, both in anticipating the future and in analysing options, is subject to intense debate and variety in practice. The sense of strategy as providing a framework for action within the organisation remains, but the means of achieving it are problematical. The traditional model of forecasting and choosing between options is simplistic in the face of uncertainty that does not yield to existing methods of prediction, and environmental complexity that is too great for existing methods of analysis. We must fall back on roles for forecasting which are exploratory and which help us to structure uncertainty, and on expectations of analysis as a diagnostic tool that assists judgment and in no sense replaces it.

If we add to this the observations of Mintzberg[16] and Rhenman[17] on the process of developing strategy, then we begin to approach a more realistic and managerially relevant sense of corporate strategy. Mintzberg's evidence points strongly to a process of strategy development which is intermittent, episodic and incident-based. Managers do not conceive of strategy either in '*a priori*' terms or as something which is developed systematically in the light of new opportunities.

Moreover, strategy does not arise merely from the reflections of 'top' managers. There is an upward flow of values and opportunities, and of perspectives on issues and problems, which substantially helps to form the strategy of the organisation. These observations push us towards the idea of strategy as a structuring force in the organisation, which defines what are relevant problems and how and by whom they are to be tackled. As Rumelt puts it: 'A principal function of strategy is to structure a situation to separate the important from the unimportant and to define the critical sub-problems to be dealt with'.[18]

However, in contrast to corporate priorities or product choices, this structuring of a situation cannot be expected to be accepted throughout the organisation merely be virtue of being stated. Whatever the corporate view about which problems are important, others in the organisation (subjected to different pressures and information) may dissent, in their behaviour if not explicitly. Indeed, it may be an important part of the organisation's dynamic that groups within it should be pursuing sectional goals, or should be responsive to particular local views of problems. So, a strategic *perspective* (and statements of strategy in which that is embodied from time to time) can be seen as being in continuing dialogue with forces within the organisation that reflect other pressures and express other concerns.

This concept of strategy as a structuring force within an organisation allows there to be less emphasis on definitive statements of strategy, justified in terms of some hallmark of analytical quality. Consequently, it offers some relief from the problems encountered by the more obsessive analytic approaches, in that the effectiveness of strategy does not then stand or fall by its prescriptive certainty in a turbulent world. However, it does lead us into other questions more concerned with process, such as:

> how can we understand and improve that process of dialogue between strategy and other factors in the organisation?

> what characteristics and means of expressing strategy enable it to contribute to effective dialogue?

These questions are overlaid by another element in the concept of strategy, stimulated by environmental turbulence, namely the development of strategic management, with its emphasis on organisational capability and learning.

STRATEGIC MANAGEMENT, CAPABILITY AND LEARNING

While the pressures of turbulence and uncertainty lead away from reliance on naive analysis and toward more concern with strategic insight in guiding the organisation, this is very much a matter of moving along a spectrum of emphasis rather than a revolutionary shift. The idea of strategic management represents a much more radical adjustment in both the focus and style of strategic concerns. Once again Ansoff crops up as a major contributor.[19]

The central assumption of strategic management (in this sense) is that adaptation of the external linkages alone is inadequate for the strategic changes that are required to cope with turbulent environments. It is also necessary to make deliberate and planned changes in the internal capability of the organisation. In strategic planning the intention was to select products or markets to play to the organisation's strengths. In strategic management, those strengths (and weaknesses) of the organisation need to be transformed to expand the adaptive opportunities available to the organisation. Moreover, the transformation of external linkages and internal capabilities must be handled in tandem and congruently if the full effect is to be achieved. Environmental challenges that exceed evolving capability must be deferred or buffered until the requisite transformation in capability has taken place. But a continually lagging capability will limit the organisation's power to defer or buffer repeatedly and the organisation may experience constant disruption as a result. Planning finds a distinctive new role in the systematic transformation of both strategy and capability. It becomes bound up inextricably with the management of real change within the organisation rather than merely concerned with strategic picture painting.

The shift of planning from a preoccupation with strategic analysis to one with change and development within the organisation involves a leap in perspective. The practical implications of the gap between the two perspectives are illustrated in Goldstein's[20] distinction between 'resource-conversion planning' and 'system improvement planning'. 'Resource-conversion planning' is 'concerned with ensuring that the primary task of an organisation will get done'. It is recognisable in terms of its major components which are forecasting, the formulation and implementation of objectives and strategies, resource planning, organisational design and organisational control. It is based in a philosophy which Goldstein calls 'planning by dominant coalition', to reflect its relation to the power structure of the organisation, and its foundation in a desire for organisational stability and consensus.

'System-improvement planning' on the other hand is concerned to ensure that the organisation and its systems, including planning, are continually being improved. It has two components – organisational learning and proactive learning. It admits of a variety of approaches to planning, being more concerned to focus learning and improvement than to conform to any abstract concept of what planning 'truly' is. Indeed planning itself is a major subject for learning and improvement.

Now the essence of Goldstein's argument is that, while both are necessary to effective organisational planning, the 'dominant coalition' philosopy, which underpins resource-conversion, is often antithetical to system-improvement planning. A commitment to improvement undermines the existing stability, and may be inconsistent with the analytical-intellectual models on which that sense of stability is based. There is, in short, an underlying tension between the philosophy and perspective of planning which seeks to bring order and structure through forecasting and strategic analysis, and that which seeks to improve the organisation's capacity to respond. This tension between analytical and developmental perspectives is a recurrent theme in this literature of alternative purposes of planning.

A similar contrast appears in Friedman's identification of alternative styles of planning.[21] He distinguishes *allocative* planning, in which the primary concern is determining patterns of resource use, *innovative* planning, where specific changes in system behaviour are being promoted, and *transactive* planning, where the determination of concerns and mutual learning between dissenting groups is the major focus. These three forms of planning are clearly appropriate to quite different assumptions about the organisation and its predicament – about the clarity and acceptability of its dominant values, about the stability and analytic tractability of the environment, and so on. Equally, planning that conformed to one rather than another of these styles could be regarded as having a different role and purpose within the organisation.

The implications of transactive modes of planning for the organisations and individuals involved are discussed by Michael.[22] He identifies specifically the personal, interpersonal and organisational burdens of involvement in planning for change. So, for example, he cites among these personal and interpersonal burdens the need to live with uncertainty, the need to embrace the inevitability of error and to recognise the complexity of goal setting, the extent to which thinking about the future undermines the reassuring stability of existing beliefs, the intensification of role conflict and role ambiguity, and the increased emphasis upon interpersonal competence. All of these are stresses which fall upon those who are involved in planning for a changing social and political environment, particularly those who are themselves the point of interface between the organisation and its environment. A further significant area of contrast concerns the very essence of learning. While everyone believes in learning, its nature and its importance vary considerably from one approach to another. In analytic-strategic approaches, learning tends to consist of building better models or forecasts as experience unfolds. Learning in this case is relatively formal and analytic, and takes place largely *within* planning itself. Contributors who write more within the developmental tradition, tend instead to make the promotion of learning the central task of planning and to see the nature of learning as itself highly problematic. The title of Donald Michael's book – *On learning to plan and planning to learn* – is more than an effectively cute phrase. It emphasises the duality of planning and learning, and, by compressing the two components into one, the notion of learning systematically how to learn. Michael emphasises social and psychological dimensions of learning, individually and in groups, and the capabilities that are necessary to sustain effective learning. These themes are extended by Argyris and Schön[23] to explore the meaning of organisational learning.

CONCLUSIONS

A brief review such as this can do no more than lightly sketch the range of ideas and perspectives which underlie a huge arena of practice. For our purpose, the primary concern is an impressionistic one – what is the broad state of strategy and planning ideas in the private sector and how has this developed under the impact of environmental turbulence?

Without being too simplistic we may define five broad conclusions:

1 That the experience of the private sector yields no dominant model of planning and strategy. On the contrary, the basic concepts have been under stress and change in the corporate sector, giving rise to an interesting plurality of approach.

2 That, in particular, complex and unpredictable environments have undermined confidence in anyone's ability to forecast accurately and have shown up the frailties of some of the widely applied analytic tools. In turn, this has undermined traditional analytic-predictive concepts of strategy.

3 That there is increasing reliance on analysis and prediction as a means of supporting managerial judgment and debate, rather than characterising them as a precise, separate and perfectable form of management science.

4 That attention has moved towards considering the role of strategy in guiding and controlling the organisation and, in particular, the process of dialogue between strategic and other perspectives within the organisation.

5 That, most recently, a more radical challenge has come through the concept of strategic management and its concern with developing organisational capability. The emphasis on learning rather than definitive solutions to problems, and on alternative roles for planning in guiding and stimulating organisational change, reflects a greater appreciation of the nature of environments which are unpredictable, complex, and ridden by conflicts in values.

Strategy in public service organisations

If this is an accurate assessment of the evolution of concepts of strategy and planning in the corporate sector, under the stress of environmental turbulence, how, if at all, does it apply in the conditions we can expect in public service organisations?

To begin with we should consider the question whether the public sector environment is peculiarly turbulent, over and above that experienced by organisations in general. It is my impression from talking to managers in public service organisations that they commonly regard this as being the case. Both the uncertainty and the invasiveness of the environment are regarded as distinctively high due to the proximity and behaviour of the political system. This is usually an impressionistic judgment, based on little empirical evidence, and with scant recognition of the problem caused for both small and large companies by the shifts in market demand, the prolonged depression, the exchange rate variations and the massive changes in materials costs which have characterised Western economies in the 1970s and 1980s.

Perhaps the only purpose of comparing the degree of turbulence is to persuade managers of public service organisations that they are not hopelessly worse off than their counterparts in the private sector (who also experience the consequences of the political process!) and that it is worth analysing the environmental turbulence they actually face as a precursor to coping with it. There are undoubtedly distinctive characteristics of turbulence for public service organisations, which tend variously to increase or decrease the intractability of the managerial task. They can either amplify or limit the 'natural' uncertainty present in the environments of all organisations. Both types of factors are present. Whether the result is more or less turbulence is a less interesting (and important) question than the nature of the turbulence and its amenability to managerial response.

As an initial approach to a complex question, I suggest five particular dimensions of turbulence for organisations *within* the public sector.

THE STRUCTURE OF UNCERTAINTIES EXPERIENCED BY PUBLIC ORGANISATIONS AND BY MANAGERS WITHIN THEM

There are two commonly argued hypotheses under this heading:

1 That, particularly under governments of a conservative persuasion, restriction on the public sector is seen as a first and major response to economic problems, and that the public sector consequently bears an undue share of any cutbacks required by social adaptation. Uncertainty and disruptions in society in general are hence amplified in their effects on the public sector.

2 That politics itself is a disruptive process for the systems under its care and is a source of uncertainty for those who operate within

those systems. A number of characteristics of the political process are cited to support this hypothesis:

> that governments experience a 'democratic imperative' to act in response to problems even where there is little evidence to suggest that action will resolve the problem;

> that they act in an instrumental manner, seeking a policy lever to pull rather than appreciating the subtleties of change in a complex system;

> that governments invariably respond to short-term pressures.

These tendencies to short-term, inappropriate and mechanistic action inevitably produce conflict between political and managerial perspectives. Those who manage complexity within public service organisations are confronted with frequent, arbitrary and simplistic interventions from politics which destabilise, rather than give structure to their world. This is not necessarily an argument about the incompetence of politics. It is more an assertion about the conflict of politics and management within the public sector, their differences in perspective, assumptions and understanding.

TURBULENCE CREATED BY THE PUBLIC SECTOR SYSTEM FOR ORGANISATIONS WITHIN IT

In the same way that politics can create turbulence for management, so may one public sector organisation create turbulence for another by its reaction to the uncertainties that both of them face. In this context we should recall that Emery and Trist's concept of turbulence is not merely about the extent of uncertainty, but about its unpredictable amplification by the field in which the organisation is lodged. It may be that this is a phenomenon which occurs particularly in public systems. Again a number of elements are involved:

1 The existence of conventions or procedures which, while designed to serve the purposes of organisation A, restrict or influence the responses of organisation B. In the British NHS, many accounting conventions and procedures exist concerning distinctions between revenue and capital or cash flow, or requirements for reporting, which inhibit rather than aid the flexibility of response of district health authorities. They exist primarily to meet governmental concerns about central accountability and control. At the same time the districts have great difficulty in

developing systems for the management and control of their own activities.

2 An emphasis on defensive reactions by a particular organisation rather than on the needs of the whole system. The supposition is that, confronted with uncertainty, those organisations that have the power to pass uncertainty on to others tend to do so. There is substantial corroborating evidence in the relationship within the NHS between regions and districts. Regions have been known to press radical changes in resource allocation on to districts, in violation of previously agreed strategies, as a means of meeting their own resourcing targets. The problem of finding a coherent response within the new resource targets is also assumed to lie with districts.

3 The legacy of institutional rigidity. Britain, in general, is characterised by little lateral mobility between its institutions – government, industry, the public service and so on. Equally, within one area of activity, such as the NHS, professional boundaries are strong and limiting. These rigidities make more difficult Emery and Trist's remedy for turbulence, namely 'the emergence of values that have overriding significance for all members of the field'.

For reasons such as these, the nature of public sector organisations is seen to amplify uncertainty rather than to reduce or control it. Relative to the uncertainty facing the public sector system as a whole, the uncertainty facing one organisation within it is high. This, it is argued, would be a primary source of turbulence for public service organisations.

THE 'POOLING' OF RISK IN THE PUBLIC SECTOR

An argument analogous to that advanced in portfolio theory in financial management suggests that risks endured by the public sector are lower than would be experienced by an individual organisation in isolation. Portfolio theory contends that, by holding a diversified portfolio, the risk applying to one's investment can be reduced to the level of 'systematic risk', namely that which affects all securities. If, as the old saying goes, 'what you gain on the swings you lose on the roundabouts', then the holding of the whole portfolio leaves no risk. But if there remain risks which affect all assets alike, then portfolio risk cannot be reduced below that level.

Though arguments about pooling of risk in the public sector have sometimes been rather casual, there may be a sense in which the risks of one public sector organisation are uncorrelated or negatively correlated with those of others. In that case, the risk of the sector as a whole is reduced. This idea of pooling may reflect a way in which the turbulence of the public sector is less than would be faced by less widely diversified systems.

LACK OF SANCTIONS

Managers in the private sector are likely to argue that the biggest difference between the two sectors is the lack of ultimate sanctions in the public sector. If management fails in the private sector, the company loses market share, makes losses and ultimately goes out of business. While the difference can be overstated – for example managers are not necessarily more likely to be fired in the private sector – there is some truth in the observation that many public sector organisations are insulated from the sanctions imposed by market forces.

LIMITATIONS ON MANAGERIAL RESPONSES

On the other hand, much of this discussion suggests that one important characteristic of public service organisations is severe limitation on their field of responses. Particularly viewed from a managerial standpoint *within* an organisation *within* the public sector, the impression can be one of few feasible options to change or make progress. In comparison with the corporate world, this may be accentuated by the absence of a whole dimension of adaptability, namely that of market and product diversification. Since the adaptation of the company through diversification and product portfolio was such an important feature of corporate strategy, it at least raises the issue of what is left when it is absent. So at least one dimension of perceived turbulence could be seen as an overload of uncertainty and stress on a very limited range of managerial responses, giving rise to an image of managers in a futile quest to square the circle.

In my view this is unduly pessimistic and I shall come on to discuss the potential of the managerial responses available to us shortly. For the moment my concern has been to offer some pegs on which our consideration of turbulence in public service organisations can be hung.

Apart from these characteristics of the public sector and their implications for the turbulence experienced by public service organisations, there are two other major differences from the corporate system we disussed in the first part. The first, mentioned above, is the absence of product or market diversification as a means of coping with uncertainty. For the corporate system the ability to adapt by moving out of inappropriate product areas and into those that offer greater profit potential, is a major strength and a fundamental plank of the concept of strategy. Without such adaptation, in what does strategy consist? Since it is clear that most public service organisations are firmly tied to a particular area of provision, it is to say the least a pertinent question.

It is made the more so by the second major difference, namely the absence of a flow of information about the consumption of the product and satisfaction with it which arises directly and automatically from its sale. The absence of a market intelligence leaves public service organisations with a profound gap in their evaluation and control of their activities, and in assessment of their own performance. These issues might otherwise have been an important alternative basis for strategy.

Against the background of such observations, it is unlikely that the inherited approach to strategy within the NHS will be very satisfactory. Traditionally the emphasis has been on incremental service strategies, in the form of desired configurations of services to be provided at some future point of time. Though a considerable effort is going into more sophisticated methods of predicting patient flows, a somewhat naive and empirically unjustified norm of required beds per thousand population is then applied to calculate the target beds needed. But the principal objections to this 'picture-painting' approach are not technical:

It represents a primitive 'forecast and allocate' approach to strategy and planning, of the sort that has proved unsustainable in the corporate sector in a turbulent environment. With much less satisfactory information and analysis even than applied there, it is unlikely to be any more successful in the NHS.

It represents a target without any appraisal of the change necessary to its achievement. Where, for example, a substantial reduction in beds is targeted, how is this to be achieved? As the targets themselves become dominated by emergent resource constraints, the question of achievable change under resource stringency becomes critical.

Just as the corporate sector has had to adjust to the realisation that its forecasting ability and its strategic analysis is inadequate to hold a turbulent environment at bay, so must the NHS with its more naked exposure to environmental change because of the absence of opportunity for diversification. The concept of strategy must emphasise organisational capability and adaptiveness as a central feature.

A concept of strategic management

For all of these reasons the concept of strategic management, with its close interrelationship between change in the organisation's substantive activities and its organisational capabilities, seems to be even more central to the needs of public service organisations than to those of the corporate system. This is manifestly so in the NHS where the magnitude of the changes which are being demanded of it – in its resource base, in the services it provides, in its managerial practice – contrast with the inertia and lack of capacity for purposive changes which seem to characterise it. We are at the early stages of developing a concept and practice of strategic management which will enable this gap to be bridged.

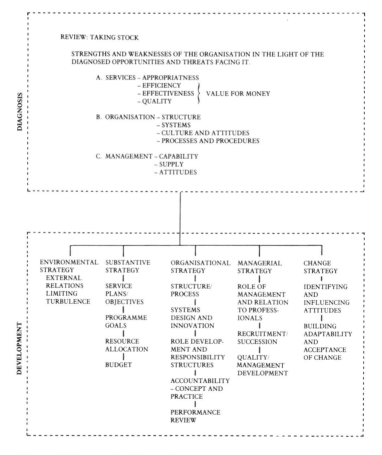

Figure 1 The strands of strategic management

Once again as a means of fixing ideas, may I present a preliminary approach to strategic management.

It depends upon a continuous learning loop:

DIAGNOSIS

DEVELOPMENT

Within this broad framework we may recognise a number of strands or elements that need to be coordinated both diagnostically and developmentally. These are outlined in Figure 1.

Now there is nothing in this scheme that is novel, except the commitment to coordinated development in response to systematic diagnosis as the basis of an organisation's strategy. The attempt to sustain that in practice will involve three further realisations:

1 The inability to manage all desirable developments concurrently. There must be priorities, but these in turn must:

a. relate back to the diagnosis of where change in capability will be most urgent or beneficial;

b. recognise the synergy between the several strands of development – for example, the mutual interdependence of innovation of systems and changes in attitudes and expectations.

2 The importance of learning and a continuous analysis (control) of the variance between expectation and outcome. This involves casting everything into the cycle of

and ensuring that the effective use of this cycle is a central part of the organisational culture.

3 The infrequency of the opportunity to make decisive change, and hence the importance of using such opportunities effectively. This gives rise to a concept of 'opportunistic strategy', which places great importance on the definition of strategic themes in a form which enables them to be pursued as opportunities arise.

More accurately, there is a need to define those development strands that can be pursued as a continuous programme and those that can be pursued only intermittently, when circumstances allow.

References

1 Drucker P. The age of discontinuity. New York, Harper and Row, 1969.
2 Toffler A. Future shock. New York, Random House, 1970.
3 For a broad summary of this intellectual schism as it applies to planning, see Best G and Evans T C. Planning. In: Wickings I (ed) Effective unit management. London, King Edward's Hospital Fund for London, 1983.
4 Emery F E and Trist E L. The casual texture of organisational environments. Human Relations, Vol 18, 1965: pp 21–32 reprinted in Emery, F E (ed) Systems thinking. London, Penguin, 1969: pp 241–257.
5 See 4: pp 249–253.
6 Andrews K R. The concept of corporate strategy. Homewood, Illinois, Irwin, 1971.
7 Ansoff H I. Corporate strategy, London, Penguin, 1968.
8 Ansoff H I. Managing surprise and discontinuity: strategic response to weak signals. California Management Review, Winter 1976.
9 Wilson I H. Forecasting social and political trends. In: Taylor Bernard and Sparkes John (eds) Corporate strategy and planning. London, Heinemann, 1977.
10 Sylvan D A and Thornson S J. Choosing appropriate techniques for socio-political forecasting. Policy Sciences, 12, 3, October 1980.
11 Cole M S D. Accuracy in the long run – where are we now? Omega, 5, 1977: pp 529–542.
12 Hedley B. Strategy and the business portfolio. Long Range Planning, 10, 1, February 1977.
13 Robinson S O Q, Hickens R E and Wade D P. The directional policy matrix – tool for strategic planning. Long Range Planning, 11, 3, 1978 *and* Hussey D E. Portfolio analysis: practical experience with the directional policy matrix. Long Range Planning, 11, 4, 1978.
14 Wensley R. The effective strategic analyst. Journal of Management Studies, 16, 3, October 1979 *and* Strategic Marketing. Betas, boxes or basics. Journal of Marketing, Summer 1981.
15 Caves R E and Porter M E. From entry barriers to mobility barriers: conjectual decisions and contrived deterrance. Quarterly Journal of Economics, May 1977.
16 Mintzberg H, Raisinghari D and Theorel A. The structure of 'unstructured' decision processes. Administrative Science Quarterly, June 1976.
17 Rhenman E Organisation theory for long range planning. Wiley, 1973.
18 Rumelt R P. Evaluation of strategy – theories and models. In Schendel D E and Hofer C W (eds) Strategic management: a new view of business policy and planning. Little Brown, 1979.

19 Ansoff H I, Declerck R P and Hayes R L. From strategic planning to strategic management. In: Ansoff, Declerck and Hayes (eds). From strategic planning to strategic management. London, John Wiley & Sons, 1976.

20 Goldstein S E. Involving managers in systems improvement planning. Long Range Planning, 14, 1, February 1981.

21 Friedman J. Retracking America: a theory of transactive planning. Anchor, 1973.

22 Michael D. On learning to plan and planning to learn. London, Jossey-Bass, 1973.

23 Argyris C and Schön, D A. Organisational learning: a theory of action perspective. Reading, MA, Addison-Wesley, 1978.

2

A New Zealand case study: Maori health

GEORGE SALMOND

Traditionally there have been three main elements in the health system in New Zealand: first, the public health services where the main concerns have been the control of infectious disease and the protection and promotion of a safe environment; second, the hospital services where the focus has been on personal care – clinical diagnosis and treatment and caring functions; and third, the community-based services centred mainly on general medical practice. In the past, each of the three elements has been largely self-contained in its mode of operation. All three have been mainly concerned with the prevention and treatment of disease rather than with the promotion of health.

Pressures now exist for major change. The determinants of health and disease are being defined more broadly. Increasingly health is being seen as everybody's business and not the exclusive preserve of health professionals. There is growing acceptance that social, cultural and economic factors profoundly influence health and disease processes. Health concerns are interwoven at all levels in society and in all sectors of the economy. Important initiatives which have a direct impact on health may exist completely outside the traditional health sector, an example being income maintenance for the disabled and the elderly. At the personal level, individuals, families, and communities are recognising that there is much they can do for themselves to promote and preserve health. The need for greater efforts in the fields of health promotion, health education and self-help health care are being pressed on all sides. Health systems managers must be responsive to all of these pressures. The balance of forces is constantly changing both within and outside the system. The issues are rarely clear cut or easy to resolve. The interested parties often have considerable freedom of action, making homogeneous strategies and concerted action difficult to achieve. Environmental turbulence and uncertainty are constant managerial companions.

To succeed it is necessary to break down strategic management into the components of a general management cycle. The relevant environments external to the organisation must be mapped. The internal environment – structure, systems, processes and beliefs and behaviours of clients and staff – must be assessed. Together these make up the diagnostic phase of the cycle. Once a diagnosis has been made and a plan has been developed, changes can be made. However, the implementation phase often is associated with a period of organisational instability which may require careful handling. In large and complex systems like health and welfare it may take some time to implement and to assess the effects of major change. Organisational learning occurs with the systematic and careful study of iterations of this management cycle.

This process of strategic management in the health sector is rarely tidy. Major components of the system exist in different phases of development. Some may be in predominantly diagnostic mode while others are trying to stabilise after a period of disruptive change. At any time changes in the external environment may require urgent strategy revision.

The following case study is mainly concerned with the environmental scanning component of the management cycle. It concerns recent efforts to improve the health of Maori people in New Zealand. The study illustrates the need for wide environmental assessment when trying to apply so called 'holistic' health concepts in the real world of health and social welfare services.

The issue

Maoris, the indigenous people in New Zealand, make up 10 per cent of the total population. It is believed that the Maori pre-European population was between 200–300,000. Diseases introduced by the Europeans and the disintegration of traditional Maori culture occasioned by European colonial activity in the 19th century resulted in a decline of the population to an estimated 42,000 by the end of the century.

By 1981, those identifying themselves as Maori in the New Zealand population had risen to 280,000 or 8.8 per cent of the total population. Three factors probably account for this increase: a high birth rate, improvements in the general standards of living, and improved use of health services – particularly public health services.

In spite of this growth, statistics still show important differences between Maori and non-Maori standards of health. Life expectancy at birth for Maoris is significantly less than for non-Maoris – for males 65.4 and 70.8 years, for females 70.0 and 77.2 years. Age adjusted Maori death rates far exceed non-Maori rates for most infectious diseases and for 'lifestyle disorders' such as heart disease, cerebrovascular disease, diabetes, alcoholism and accidents. Efforts to improve Maori health by the use of western methods have been modestly successful but, on most counts, the health status differential between Maori and non-Maori has continued to grow.

With their culture dislocated and their language suppressed, deprived of much of their land and weakened by disease, Maoris suffered from low morale at the turn of the century. As the lot of Maori people began to improve in the first half of this century the population began to grow and morale began to rise. Most of this improvement was achieved by Maori people striving to adapt themselves to the colonial culture. At least in public life, and probably in private life also, Maori matters were largely suppressed.

Over the last decade in New Zealand there has been a major renaissance of Maori culture in all of its manifestations. Maori people are demanding that their cultural knowledge, attitudes and practices be recognised and given greater prominence in all aspects of New Zealand life. The language is now widely taught in kindergartens and increasingly in schools. The Maori arts such as carving and weaving are flourishing as are the performing arts. Recently a number of large Maori-led economic enterprises and business ventures have been launched. Maori cultural practices are being observed, developed and increasingly shared with non-Maoris. In general Maori people are displaying greater confidence and pride in their Maori identity.

Health has become a focal point for this resurgence. Maori concepts of health and disease are more broadly based than most western concepts. Maori people recognise four elements in health – spiritual wellbeing (*te taha wairua*) which is all important and relates to land and ancestors; mental wellbeing (*te taha hinengero*) which concerns the cultural mind set; family wellbeing (*te taha whanau*) which incorporates family support and tribal affiliations; and physical wellbeing (*te taha tinana*) which relates to bodily health.

Maori people contend that good health can only be attained by people who have a positive sense of cultural identity and high self esteem. They believe that all four components must be in balance for health to be achieved. In their perception, the western health care system is preoccupied with physical wellbeing to the detriment of the other elements.

An environmental scan

In response to a rising tide of advocacy, the health system has taken a number of initiatives aimed at promoting Maori health. Most of the early initiatives were concerned with environmental assessment. In March 1984, a one-week residential workshop (*Te Hui Whakaoranga*) was held involving over 200 Maori and non-Maori leaders from the health and related social services and from the community. In discussion differing perceptions, attitudes and practices were shared, needs and expectations identified and plans made to continue the dialogue and to plan and implement desired changes.

Te Hui Whakaoranga identified a number of areas in which the health services are seen as deficient. However, Maori people often have difficulty in communicating their concerns and needs to non-Maori health workers not familiar with Maori attitudes and practices. So, it was agreed that ways must be found to gather, organise and share this knowledge. Where Maori healing practices are significantly different from those of the dominant culture these must be recognised and appropriate provision made. All health workers must receive some training in Maori culture and in Maori health. Resource people should be readily available to deal with difficult problems.

A strong and recurring theme at the *hui* was the wish that Maori people have for a greater say in the use of public health resources. This applies at all levels from the national level down to activity involving self-help community groups. The clear message was 'give us the resources and let us do the job – if we want help we will ask for it'. Given equitable access to health resources, Maori people feel that there is much they can do for themselves.

This new-found assertiveness presents some dilemmas for health administrators. Like other human groups, Maori society is not homogeneous and does not speak with one voice. Views differ between the young and their elders, between urban and rural Maoris, between males and females, between people with different tribal affiliations and between political conservatives and left-wing radicals. All of these views must be taken into account. There are difficulties, however.

First, the vigorous and uncompromising advocacy of some Maori activists have tended to alienate sections of the health community and of the public at large. Not everyone supports affirmative action in the interests of promoting Maori health, and questions have been raised about possible racial discrimination and separate development. 'Why', some ask, 'is it necessary to make special provision for Maori health?' 'Why won't the Maoris simply fit in like other New Zealanders?'

Second, in advancing their proposals for reform and innovation, Maori people tend to be long on concepts and advocacy but short on the abilities needed to turn ideas into practical propositions. Coming from an oral tradition, Maoris communicate much more effectively with the spoken word than they do on paper. As the Maori language becomes more widely used and educational attainment rises, communication is becoming easier but such changes can only occur slowly. Furthermore, few Maoris are well versed in the mechanisms of government and thus able to work 'the system'. Few occupy senior positions in the public services – including the health services. In general, advocacy tends to be directed to the higher political levels in the hope of prompting quick and major change. Less attention by way of steady pressure is applied at operating levels within the various bureaucracies.

Third, many of the ideas advanced by Maori people are in keeping with 'holistic' concepts of health and health care. Here there are direct parallels with the primary health care approach promoted by the World Health Organization. Health is something which is tangible, has positive value and can be promoted as an integral part of social and economic development. Health care is not an isolated activity concerned with clinical diagnosis and the treatment of disease. To be fully effective not only must care be based on sound science, it must also be culturally congruent and grounded in the principles of self-help and self-reliance. Maori health initiatives embody all of these concepts.

Despite being in good currency philosophically, though, holistic health care concepts are not easily accommodated within the existing health and welfare systems. To implement many of the Maori health proposals would require significant changes in the systems of government and in the way the bureaucracy works. Gradually, in response to a wide variety of pressures changes are taking place. In this sense Maori health is in the forefront of health services development. An environmental scan of almost any aspect of health care in New Zealand at the present time cannot afford to ignore developments in Maori health.

Evolving a strategy

The past two years have seen a number of developments which could be seen as strands in an evolving strategy for Maori health. In summary these are as follows.

1 *Structural changes*

establishment, by the national Board of Health, of a standing advisory committee, of mainly Maori people, on Maori health;

establishment, within the Department of Health, of an advisory committee, of mainly Maori officers, on Maori health;

creation within the Division of Health Promotion of a section on Maori health;

appointment of Maori community health workers to work with public staff in many health districts;

appointment of Maori health liaison officers by a number of hospital boards.

2 *Systems changes*

hospital boards and district health offices have organised their own health *huis* at which health politicians, administrators and clinicians have met with the local Maori people;

a community health initiatives funding scheme has been introduced to finance and otherwise support self-help groups involved in health related activity – a number of Maori groups have been supported;

a national health promotion programme mainly involving young Maori people has been funded – activities range from programmes on national television to cultural events, Maori games and self-help community development projects;

some psychiatric hospitals have set aside facilities to be run along Maori lines by mainly Maori staff for Maori patients;

research projects have been carried out on Maori healing practices, the health of Maori women and the high rate of post-neonatal death among Maori infants.

3 *Workforce changes*

interested health workers have been encouraged to learn the Maori language;

cultural awareness courses have been held in traditional Maori settings for health workers interested and involved in Maori health;

training courses have been established for Maori community health workers;

the Maori health component of basic training has been strengthened for many health workers;

affirmative action programmes have been established to recruit, train and retain Maori people in health employment.

Conclusion

Classification of these strands in terms of strategic management is difficult because of their interweaving. The pace of change both within and beyond the health system is such that constant environmental scanning is needed. The management task is to keep track of what is happening on a broad front, to be sensitive and responsive to the environmental influences, to guide the development and implementation of the strategy and to integrate its component parts, to seek out and take advantage of opportunities to advance the strategy, to weather the inevitable turbulence and to encourage the organisation and the people within it to learn from the experience and grow.

3

Financing cross-subsidized products in a price-competitive environment

RICHARD M KNAPP

> The winners in this game are buyers who get more for less and
> sellers who capture patients and transform services into capital.
> In this game the winners survive and the losers go bankrupt.

This is how Dr William S Kiser, Chief Executive Officer of the
Cleveland Clinic, characterized the American medical marketplace in his 1984 address to the American Urological Association.
The hospital business in the United States is clearly becoming
more competitive, with price becoming its driving force. While
cooperation and community responsibility have been hallmark
values and attitudes of the past, the current competitive environment is developing a new set of attitudes and values. Community
planning has been replaced by strategic planning, survival of the
institution is seen as an organizational objective rather than a
means to an end, and information, management techniques, and
organizational structures are beginning to be viewed as corporate
assets to be protected rather than shared.

The increase in the supply of highly trained physicians is
intensifying competition between groups of physicians and
hospitals for the provision of all services, particularly capital
intensive services. Traditional relationships of patient-provider-
insurer are being disrupted as large-scale purchasers (self-insured
corporations or variously titled alternative delivery systems) in-
tervene in the determination of where and how their covered
populations receive care.

The changing business environment

Deregulation and a return to price competition is a phenomenon
that is intensifying throughout the American economy. The most
obvious examples include the communications, airline, and banking sectors. While benefits to the overall change in philosophy
and operation of these industries have been given much attention,
there are adverse side-effects which also need to be understood.
Stories are beginning to appear in the media which are drawing
attention to these side-effects. A notable example was a report in a
September 1984 issue of *The Washington Post* entitled, 'Saving

those wounded in our deregulation frenzy'. While not stated directly in this way, the theme of that report was that whenever price becomes a dominant force in the marketplace, all cross-subsidized products and services come to the surface for attention. For example, in the business sectors cited earlier, long distance telephone service subsidized local services, high volume and high mileage routes subsidized low volume airline routes, and personal checking account services were subsidized by other profitable banking services. Prices for these cross-subsidized services have begun to rise rapidly as competition has been introduced into other high volume markets where the subsidies were borne.[1]

To the degree that some of the cross-subsidized services are viewed as necessary personal services for large groups in the population who cannot afford them, they will become serious political issues in the future. For example, home telephone service and a personal checking account may be right behind food stamps and subsidized fuel as issues which command political attention. The subsidized pricing structure of the past assured that most individuals could afford these services. The eroding ability to cross-subsidize the production of these services in future will bring attention to them, and a debate will ensue as to how these services should be financed and provided for those who cannot afford them.[2]

Implications for health services

What has all this to do with hospitals, doctors and health services generally? Notwithstanding the previously held views that the medical marketplace is not responsive to traditional economic theory, we are learning that the forces of supply, demand and price do make a difference in the health services marketplace. It is true that price does not have to be *the* dominant force in the environment. Thoughtful observers have pointed out that Kodak is not the low priced photographic film nor is Budweiser the low priced beer[3], even though both brands dominate their respective markets. However, the industry-wide cross-subsidized products which were highlighted in the previous section of this paper do have important analogies in the health care field. To a major extent these analogies exist largely in the nation's medical center teaching hospitals.

There are at least four cross-subsidized products or services which can be identified in the American medical marketplace:

specialized standby services;
uncompensated care;
clinical education in the health sciences;
provision of an environment for clinical research.

While there are over 1500 institutions in the United States which participate in graduate medical education, only 117 of these are hospitals which may be classified as academic medical center hospitals on the basis of the fact that the majority of chairmen in the medical school either serve as the hospital clinical chief of service or have the prerogative of appointing the hospital chief of service. While there are wide variations in their organization and functions, these 117 hospitals represent the extreme end of the continuum when it comes to the scope and intensity of service programs; provision of specialized standby services; uncompensated care obligations; the size and scope of medical residency and fellowship programs, as well as other educational programs; and commitment to an environment in which clinical research will flourish.

'Cost shifting' is a term that is used to describe the circumstances when an individual is provided with services, but the cost of doing so is shifted to another payer because that individual either cannot or will not pay for the services. This term has been used largely to describe the phenomenon of uncompensated care. However, there are other types of cost shifting that occur in hospital financial arrangements. They are more commonly referred to as cross-subsidies, but the principle is the same. The special standby services, the distinctive diagnostic case mix of teaching hospital patients, the costs of education, and the provision of a clinical research environment are all subsidized for the most part using patient care revenue from routine patients.

SPECIALIZED AND STANDBY SERVICES

The teaching hospital's patient care reputation is clear: it is the place for the most severely ill patients. Teaching hospitals are the primary care source of microsurgery, joint replacement surgery, transplant surgery, specialized laboratory and blood banking services, and specialized neurological and ophthalmologic procedures to name a few. Patients with the most severe medical needs tend to be sent to teaching hospitals with the most advanced health care capabilities.

While the charges for many of these services are related to the costs of providing them, there are some services for which special charges are not made, or for which charges are not set high enough to cover full costs. For example, at many medical center hospitals, services are provided to a very substantial number of high risk pregnant women. The cost of providing services to these women is substantially higher than the cost of providing service to women whose pregnancies are without substantial risk. In most hospitals the charges for services to these two groups of women are substantially the same, even though the costs of providing these services are quite different. In effect, the patients with extensive needs are being subsidized by the patient with routine needs because the charges are based on averages. As a result, in a market where patients are sensitive to hospital prices, the teaching hopital is at a disadvantage. It should not be surprising to see teaching hospitals in response begin to set prices for standby services and other tertiary care services at a rate which more clearly is related to the actual costs of providing such services, and the public will have to become used to paying much more for services which had been subsidized in the past.

A number of researchers are presently developing indices to measure severity of illness and intensity of service. If successful, these efforts may improve price comparisons between hospitals and legitimate price differentials within hospitals. These efforts are particularly important to teaching hospitals since the teaching hospital serves more intensively ill patients and at the same time provides a substantial number of standby services. Until such research efforts provide a practical way to measure these variations, the average cost and charge of teaching hospitals will be higher than the average cost and charge for non-teaching hospitals.

UNCOMPENSATED CARE

Major amounts of uncompensated care are presently being provided by some American hospitals. The expenses necessary for this care – staff, supplies, facilities, and equipment – are already in the present hospital system. The financing of those services is a hodge-podge of cost shifting, philanthropy, lost earnings and appropriations. Nonetheless, hospitals have been able until recently to provide significant amounts of uncompensated care without significant loss. What is most at risk in the changing business environment is that the self-focused cost containment efforts of individual third party payers will silently squeeze the present level of funding for uncompensated care out of the system. The increases in the price consciousness of buyers of hospital services place hospitals with large uncompensated care burdens at a significant and growing disadvantage. In the absence of a comprehensive entitlement program for financing health services of the poor and medically indigent, hospitals historically have set their prices to subsidize uncompensated care with funds from their paying patients, where possible. In a marketplace of price sensitive consumers, hospitals which now attempt this cost shifting to underwrite uncompensated care will be at a significant disadvantage. Their necessarily higher prices will make them less attractive to paying patients and, as paying patients choose cheaper hospitals without the uncompensated care surcharge, the financial problem of the hospital with a major uncompensated care burden will get worse and worse.

The conclusion of these observations is clear: uncompensated care is a major problem in a competitive environment because uncompensated care is unevenly distributed across hospitals. This uneven distribution in a competitive market handicaps hospitals serving the indigent and medically indigent and benefits hospitals with primarily paying patients. As Princeton Professor Uwe Reinhardt has stated: 'To saddle providers of indigent care with the dual responsibility of first, treating uninsured indigents, and second, casting about for a private source that can be focused to pay for such care strikes one as a dubious social policy, particularly when the burden of that care is so unevenly distributed among hospitals.' Given current trends, and the unevenly distributed burden of providing uncompensated care, it seems clear that if substantial changes are not made, the US shall return to a two-class system of hospital and medical services, and access to services for those who cannot afford to pay for them will be severely curtailed.

CLINICAL EDUCATION IN THE HEALTH SERVICES

Teaching hospitals are major educational institutions. The clinical education of medical, nursing and allied health students is organized around the daily operations of the hospitals. Patients are being treated and students are being trained through the same activities. In effect, both products – patient care and education – are being produced simultaneously, or jointly. The joint nature of patient services and clinical education does *not* imply that education is being produced without additional costs – education is *not* simply a byproduct. The addition of the educational role does involve additional costs for supervising faculty, clerical support, physical facilities, lowered productivity, and increased ancillary service use. It is most difficult, however, to identify distinctly many of the educational costs because of the impossibility of a clear separation of clinical care from clinical education. It is also difficult to quantify the service benefits teaching hospitals receive from physicians, nurses, and technicians in training programs.

For example, medical residents learn clinical skills through supervised participation in the diagnosis and care of patients. The patient service benefits that accompany this learning reduce, in some part, the costs of graduate medical education programs. The cost reduction varies with the patients' clinical needs and the residents' level of training. Service benefits provided by residents are probably more substantial for tertiary care patients requiring continuous medical supervision than for routine patients and are greater for senior residents than junior residents. While there is no conclusive study comparing the costs added by residency programs with the service benefits provided by residents, hospital executives and medical educators generally believe that the costs of operating educational programs exceed the service benefits obtained by patients. This added cost is the investment necessary to adequately prepare the future generation of professional health personnel, and its inclusion in hospital prices disadvantages teaching hospitals in a price sensitive market.

CLINICAL RESEARCH

In the past four decades, the medical sciences have made dramatic advances in diagnosis and treatment. Much that is now widely available was unknown a generation or two ago. Many of these advances began in the basic research laboratories of universities and their affiliated hospitals; most of the advances were transferred to patient care as clinical research programs at teaching hospitals.

The presence of medical research in the teaching hospital has environmental, managerial and financial implications. To attract and retain research-oriented faculty physicians, the hospital must create and maintain a climate conducive to research. Research scholarship must be esteemed, research support and supplies must be readily available, and individual hospital departments must be flexible and responsive to the demands accompanying research. Managerially, the inclusion of medical research in a teaching hospital's primary mission requires governing board and senior management commitment to integrating research into the daily operations of the hospital. Specialized supporting staff must be hired and trained, necessary review and patient-protection procedures must be developed and monitored, record-keeping and reporting procedures for the funding organization must be established, and management styles appropriate for personalized and efficient patient care must be balanced with collegial style appropriate for research productivity. Without an appropriate environment and management, research will not flourish.

Establishing a medical research program increases a teaching hospital's costs. Additional costs are incurred for staff, supplies and equipment, space, maintenance and upkeep, and record-keeping. Most, but not all, of these added costs are supported by grants, contracts, endowments and gifts. Regular hospital services provided for research patients are paid generally by the patient or his third party coverage. However, consider the necessary attributes of a first-class research environment:

a slower pace of operation;
the necessity of academic rewards and symbols;
tolerance of low volume services, particularly in 'tertiary care' areas;
tolerance of clinical diversity; and
space, equipment, and other capital outlays for academic purposes.

Match these attributes to the incentives in the newly emerging price competitive environment:

increased admissions and patient turnover;
avoidance/closure of low volume/high cost services;
specialization in 'profitable' program areas; and
reduction in length of stay, ancillary service use, cost of labor, supplies and capital.

There is much to be said and understood about this subject. However, the point that needs to be made is that without an appropriate environment and management attitude, research simply will not flourish.

Concluding observations

A substantial portion of this paper has been devoted to a description of the societal contributions of medical center teaching hospitals. This has been done to be sure certain questions receive proper attention. In a broad societal context, the question becomes, 'Will certain desirable functions be continued?' Under both regulated and marketplace models, price competition is the present emphasis and the unique and important teaching hospital contributions are disadvantaged by the pricing implications of the new environment. Whether we move in the direction of competition or regulation, it is easy to say, 'Sure, clinical research will move ahead, new tertiary services will be available, manpower will be trained and educated, and someone will take care of the poor.' Those words roll out so easily and, more recently, with greater and greater frequency. However, the financing arrangements and characteristics of the hospital environment which have enabled us to support these important societal contributions of the teaching hospitals are beginning to shift, and changes are occurring rapidly.

With the exception of research grants and contracts, and state and local government support for a relatively small number of hospitals, patient service revenue in the teaching hospital is the financial source of support for these very necessary societal contributions. Essentially, what we are doing in the US is subsidizing several functions with revenue from one function. However, these cross-subsidy choices are less and less available as the environment changes to reflect an attitude where competition is strictly on the basis of price. Suffice it to say that although price competition may stimulate prudent decisions by educated consumers and groups with purchasing power, there are not assurances that those 'dollar votes' will result in a medical service system that will achieve the nation's health care goals and meet the needs of all our citizens.

References

1 Quinn J B. The big breakup: a report card. Newsweek, 21 January, 1985: p 61.
2 Horwitz S. Phone, banking lifelines sought for nation's poor. The Washington Post, 10 March, 1985.
3 Vladeck B C. The dilemma between competition and community service, Inquiry, XXII, 2, Summer 1985: p 115.

4

The local dimension: care in the community

DAVID KING

It must be our addiction to the newspaper headline which attracts us to those pithy one liners summing up life, or characterising a social trend we can sense but not express until we have that invaluable latchkey of a few words to unlock meaning. 'Small is beautiful' and 'the medium is the message' are two examples: they seem to say it all in exactly the way we would have done so ourselves had we coined the phrase first. Saying it briefly, mysteriously leaves nothing more to be said; it is elegantly self evident. Self evident, that is, until someone – usually a child – demands a fuller explanation and then the fun starts. That clear meaning we could sense can become as slippery as an eel when we attempt to amplify what it is intended to convey. For me, and I suspect for many others, 'care in the community' is a prime example of an aphorism so abundantly clear in general terms, but so elusive in detail. It is a relative newcomer to health language in the UK but is so full of intended and unintended meaning that its very utterance can unite or divide company in the most dramatic way.

It marks a watershed in the trend of healthcare provision and trying to discover its meaning and translate it into action has occupied my professional life these past fifteen years. There is no other concept of such strategic importance. Before it came on the scene, thinking, training, clinical and managerial activity were influenced by a diametrically opposed philosophy. It was one which lauded centralism justified by the benefits of 'economies of scale', 'critical mass', 'centres of excellence'. Such ideas were ingrained at the outset of my career which commenced in a London teaching hospital where the view was unconsciously inculcated that, of all the sick, the lucky ones were those safely in its beds and close to its life preserving and enhancing qualities. Care in the community as an alternative for any of its activities could only be regarded as cheap, nasty, and negligent. It was not until 1970, or thereabouts, that it was first suggested to me that some of the work we had so painstakingly centralised in the name of excellence and benefit to patients was inappropriate, wasteful, counter-productive, misconceived, even harmful. The message seemed important, but marginal. However, as the years go on so there seem to be ever more aspects of health services which have been centralised and now cry out to be distributed locally. What follows is a case study which describes some of the devices that have been employed to inform a local debate in my district about where services are best located. It also describes how the notions of care in the community increasingly affect what we do, as managers.

The setting

Exeter is a health district in the south west of England, it is 60 miles east to west, and 30 miles north to south with a population of 300,000, some 20 per cent of whom are over 65. The city of Exeter (100,000 population) has a university and is the local government centre for the County of Devon (1 million population, including the Exeter district). Some aspects of health care were once undertaken by counties, and Exeter has traditionally been the site for a number of services – principally the big psychiatric hospitals. But Devon has four health authorities and they are all keen to be as self sufficient as possible. Within the Exeter district there are a number of small towns – seaside resorts, agricultural markets, and a port. Several of them have local hospitals as well as primary care services. When the district was formed in 1974, there was widespread concern that the small hospitals would close because the economic and medical orthodoxy of the day was that such places were unsafe and expensive. Plans existed to replace them either by services in Exeter or by fewer and larger community hospitals. Although these plans had not been declared publicly, they were suspected by the local population and in consequence health authorities and their administrators were not trusted.

This is a prosperous society, one which pays its taxes but, unlike the popular stereotype, does not leave it all to the state. There is strong local pride in each community which is expressed in gifts of time and resources for enterprises identified by local leaders. Each local hospital has a League of Friends which will provide voluntary service to the patients and vigorously collect money for equipment or building schemes.

It was to this atmosphere I was introduced when appointed district administrator in 1974. My previous experience in a similarly scattered rural area had alerted me to some of the insensitive demands of centralisation. One example of this was the location of the area's hearing aid spares replacement service on one site, which meant that old people had to make long journeys to replace batteries or the cheapest component. I was alert to such problems but felt that their solution was best left to professionals.

1974–1979: No more than a beginning

Before 1974 the statutory health services in Exeter had been managed by five separate authorities: three for the hospitals and two for the domiciliary and public health services. Together they comprised nearly all the NHS provision, only the family doctor service was administered separately. With the 1974 reorganisation, these separate authorities were to work in close cooperation.

The marriage was not one of equals. In Exeter about 90 per cent of the health budget was spent on hospitals and in consequence there was real concern that hospital issues would predominate. We sought to establish a management structure in which the forces of centralisation and decentralisation would have comparable voice by setting up two main units of management, one to run the central hospitals (1150 beds) and the other to manage the local services, including the local hospitals (10 in number with 470 beds).

Progress in a number of services was not as rapid as we might have wished in the first five years, but for the elderly things did get better. Of the eight towns outside Exeter in which there were hospitals, only in three were there long stay beds for the elderly. This meant that many old people were admitted for long stay care to hospitals 20 or 30 miles from home: bad enough if there was public transport, very depressing if there was none to bring the occasional familiar face from home. This was also the time when day hospitals for the elderly were just being introduced and there were two in the district in 1975. The conditions of some of the conventional hospital wards for old people were scandalous. We managed by dint of of persuasive argument and persistence to do something about all three matters. There are now long-stay beds in all eight centres, day hospitals in seven of them, and Charles Dickens would only feel at home in one or two wards now – I am still ashamed to say. However, because it is not a common expectation that local services will develop and improve, these changes have been very popular.

1979–1984: Discovering the community

The second five years have been more fruitful. Many factors have influenced the change and it is worth giving some account of each of them before describing their combined effect on the way we do business now.

MORE LOCALITIES

There was no particular logic in simply concentrating on the localities which already had hospitals and, in any case, others were knocking on the door and asking for better services. What was an appropriate size of locality to recognise for planning and service provision? Despite the logic of the case to identify more communities, I must confess to having experienced a personal reluctance to opening up more territories with their own ambitions and demands on our limited resources – it felt too much like making additional work for ourselves. Even so, we were eventually driven by the force of our own arguments so that not only have we recognised more localities, but have put no limit on the final number we could consider.

THE BREAKOUT FROM THE PSYCHIATRIC HOSPITALS

In addition to all the services mentioned, Exeter managed about 3000 psychiatric hospital beds (mental illness and mental handicap) in 1974. These served not only the Exeter district but four others too. Until 1979 we tried to improve the service in existing hospitals while decentralising services (including the funds for them) back to the client districts. Because we were trying to move in two directions simultaneously, it is hardly surprising that there was little progress. In 1979 we decided to close our hospitals and create community services in the client districts and in Exeter too. The scale of resource redistribution (£23m revenue and 2500 staff) and the speed of change has made this publicly the best known of our programmes.

LEARNING MORE ABOUT PEOPLE

There is a tendency in health services to regard sick and disabled people as helplessly dependent. We assess their functional disabilities and do our best to compensate for them, but this usually leads to greater dependence rather than rehabilitation. It is not what people want when you ask them. They do not consider that their disabilities should disqualify them from life, but that they should be compensated by appropriate help and facilities so that they can get on and lead their own lives. Many people who formerly appeared helpless and in need of institutional support could be independent with some help at home. We were denied these lessons when we were confined to managing hospitals; they only became clear to us when we worked more in the community.

LEARNING MORE ABOUT THE COMMUNITY

Officials in statutory services tend to assume that what they do not provide, does not exist. We have discovered how mistaken this is and how resourceful a local community can be in providing for its needs. The major contribution of care is given by one individual to another usually within the family. There has been a considerable research effort in the UK to assess the irreplaceable role of the 'informal carer'. We are also impressed by the amount and variety of voluntary services there are, often organised at a fraction of the cost we incur. Of course, all this was going on before, but we concentrated on our hospitals and were blind to it.

THE COMMUNITY HEALTH COUNCIL (CHC)

In 1974 a CHC was formed in each health district to be a public watchdog. We formed a robust friendship with our watchdog and I believe it has been the most influential factor in effecting the transition from the reserved, 'behind closed doors' existence health authorities lead before 1974, to the rough and tumble of open debate. The CHC has done an excellent job in introducing the public and health authority to each other.

Locality planning

In 1981 we concluded that trying to think and plan community services on a district basis was fruitless and the time had come to recognise that just as the district was the appropriate context for developing central hospital services, we needed a local context for developing community services. We instituted something we have called 'locality planning' which is nothing more complex than using the knowledge and experience of local people to shape the most appropriate services for their neck of the woods. It is more an attitude of mind than a technique. In a sense the idea found us and so we decided not to impose a new system but let one develop pragmatically. There was a danger that we would impose rules for the recognition of localities – arbitrary population size, for example – when they were natural entities which would identify themselves rather than be defined administratively. So far there are 14 localities varying in population from 10,000 to 40,000.

The picture is vastly different from the days of our original eight hospital locations. A review of some old plans indicates that nine years ago we were trying to find ways of reducing the number of centres for local services, not increasing them. There is one locality which is small and distant from Exeter and which without this change of thinking would have had a totally different deal, because prior to locality planning we were forever saying that the area was too small for us to make 'viable' provision.

If the definition of localities seems a little haphazard, it is a model of administrative order compared with the variety of meetings and how people join them to discuss and advise on local needs. The health authority has set up locality planning teams comprised mainly of locally based professional staff from health and other local government services. But there are also local councillors, representatives of voluntary organisations and anyone whose work in the locality suggests they would have a contribution to make. Local teams have also been formed to plan and manage the new service for mentally handicapped people which is being developed. We are particularly anxious to involve consumers in this and so there are members of the teams nominated by the families receiving service. The CHC has established a health forum in a number of localities to inform it of the particular local needs of that community. There is no shortage of channels to inform the concensus of what needs to be done in each community.

RESULTS

Here are a number of things that have happened as a consequence of locality planning:

1 A shortfall of geriatric beds for the district was to have been met by building a new ward block at the central hospital. Instead of this, the two communities which largely account for the need are to have their own local provision and will for the first time become service centres. In effect, we shall be opening new cottage hospitals.

2 The whole service for the confused elderly, formerly located in one of the mental hospitals, is to be distributed over 12 localities. Each will have its own beds, day and domiciliary provision for the first time. This exercise more than any other has demonstrated that small, local units offer better value for money because of the immensely high overheads of the large psychiatric hospitals. In the new service these overhead costs can be invested in care, not in the heating and maintenance of mile long corridors and spacious, unused ballrooms.

3 Mental health centres are being established across the district so that people will no longer have to travel to Exeter for outpatient and day facilities.

4 Similar local provision is being made for people with mental handicap. The original plan is being modified daily by experience so that the service grows more flexible and consumer orientated.

5 Local domiciliary schemes for the care of terminally ill people have been supported in preference to a central hospice.

6 One town had long wanted a day centre for its mentally handi-capped residents and had been offered the standard 60-place version in a 'long-term' plan. Instead, it is now to get something this year for the actual 20–30 mentally handicapped people who live in the town. We have bought a large old house for the purpose and the families of the mentally handicapped will help in setting it up. This is a good example of how we can weather local controversy because we are known and not a distant bureaucracy. The plan to substitute the smaller day centre for an architect-designed version incensed the local county councillor who con-ducted a press campaign against the idea, until at a meeting with families she could see that it was their wish to get something done and that this was not a decision foisted on them.

Temporary conclusions

We are all programmed in our basic and professional training with concepts of current orthodoxy, unchallenged tenets of faith. Reviewing my own, it seems that I was too imbued with the inevitability and necessity of centralisation so that when 'care in the community' was first suggested as an alternative I was set to reject it. It seemed basically impractical: to appreciate its possi-bilities and put them into effect has required a fundamental shift in attitude. For all its slightness and imperfections 'locality plan-ning' has facilitated that change in thinking and has thereby altered the way we provide services, their style and distribution.

It has its critics who tell us that it is a method only appropriate to scattered rural populations. Certainly, it is in the country communities that it has best succeeded and its application in the city has been slow: it would be good to see the idea tried in a big city. There are concerns expressed that because we are involved in the selection of representatives on the local teams the process is not democratic. Still others complain that real work is best done with much smaller territories and populations: a neighbourhood block with at most one or two thousand inhabitants. Perhaps we shall refine our focus in the next few years to concentrate atten-tion on smaller populations. Another comment frequently made is that the method may be useful for those aspects of health services that some call 'care' – support for long-term, chronic conditions – but irrelevant for the 'cure' or secondary acute services.

Ten years ago I would not have predicted that our professional attitudes about location of services could be so fundamentally influenced by local debate, though there is still much to be done to show in real terms that things have actually changed on the ground and not just in our thinking. It will be interesting to see where we are in the next five and ten years and whether the changes will be as radical as those in the last decade.

Planning strategy

Introduction

The focus of this section is on how strategy is formed. This sub-theme raises several immediate questions, like 'What is strategy?' and 'Why does a manager need strategy?' and, if those can be answered, 'How does the manager know if his or her strategy is any good?' During the international seminar, much of the discussion around these issues concentrated on the notion that *how* decisions are made affects *what* decisions are made. As a result, the processes by which a manager's strategy are formed could be important determinants of what the strategies will be.

Among the most common of the processes that organisations conventionally employ in the formulation of their strategies is strategic planning. Yet strategic planning in some organisations is regarded as an activity or function peripheral to the central role of the manager. In those organisations, strategy is something that managers get on with implementing once higher-level policy-makers or lower-level staff people have written the strategic plan. This separation of planning from implementation has real dangers of reifying strategic decision-making as something different from management. It raises the worrying concern of who then is responsible for managing the ever-changing interface between the organisation and its environment. If these dangers are to be avoided, planning can not be divorced from management, and managers need to see planning as an integral part of what they do.

Greg Parston's introductory paper on this sub-theme argues that planning, implementation and change are not discrete or sequential phases of managing an organisation, but that they are interactive and simultaneous activities. In this context, planning should contribute its analytical and explorative capacities to organisational learning and to the development and management of strategies, rather than being simply a formalized process of plan-production.

Beginning by exploring what is meant by strategy, the paper reasons that what strategy is – whether a plan or guidelines or some other form – depends upon the environmental and organisational conditions which confront the manager at the time. Some managers, however, risk failure by assuming that current strategies fit even though conditions have changed. This results in part because those managers fail to monitor, to analyse and to explore environmental and organisational change. They are not using planning to learn. But an organisation's planning process itself also can contribute to a lack of strategic fit by regularly producing standardised strategies that have little to do with what the organisation currently needs. Parston cites examples that underscore the importance of an ongoing analysis of the interaction between an organisation's strategy and the factors to which it is meant to respond, and concludes by proposing that planning what planning's role should be is an important responsibility of the strategic manager.

The interaction of strategic planning and other management activities is highlighted in the papers that are written by health services managers. Sandy Macpherson's case study shows that careful environmental analysis is crucial to development of strategy, as well as to its chances for successful implementation. The AIDS epidemic is a significant health problem in the City of Toronto. Formulating a coordinated public health response to the epidemic entails educational and political initiatives with various groups in the environment, each with their own sets of concerns. As these initiatives have effect, planning with those groups what their own responses will be serves as an important process by which the City's overall strategy is being implemented.

Bob Dearden's paper describes the process by which a new organisation's strategic plan is developed. The National Health Service Training Authority was created to take on previously dispersed responsibilities for training and education in the NHS. The process of producing the NHSTA's first plan had to be sensitive to the many vested interests and constraining factors in the environment. This was important not just because it made good planning sense, but because the process of planning contributed significantly to the establishment, legitimation and development of the new organisation. The personal lessons for the manager from this experience are several, as Dearden concludes with some insightful observations about the process and context of planning strategic change.

Another aspect of the link between strategic planning and organisational development is explored in Duncan Nichol's paper. He examines how the difficulties of a district health authority in the UK presented a need for both an alternative approach to planning and an improvement in the organisation's general capacity to respond to change. Planning served as a good vehicle for organisational development because of its broad impact on people working in many parts of the organisation – authority members, district and unit managers, and clinicians, among them. The case study is used to demonstrate how important it is for managers to design the linkages between what the organisation plans to do substantively and the systems, processes and management capacities that they must develop in order to achieve it.

These manager's reflections show clearly that, like the problems they face, their own work is not tidy. Managers' problems lack order; the responses to them cannot be the methodical sequence of steps nor the application of platitudes that some would have us believe. Managers manage messes. In order to do that well, they have to be able to recognize the need for their own activities to overlap, they have to seize threats that can be made into opportunities, and they have to understand when process is more important than task.

5

Learning to use plans and guidelines

GREG PARSTON

Strategy is not simply a plan. Strategic planning, though, more frequently produces a plan than a strategy. A manager who confuses a plan for strategy, when it is not one, can incur great risks, sometimes fails as a result, and frequently blames poor planning. The real fault for failure, though, may rest on a confusion about what strategy is, about what planning should do in an organisation, and thus about what the manager is using planning for.

This paper puts forward a framework for further consideration of strategy and of strategic planning. It attempts to string together three sets of ideas which too often are treated separately: what strategy is; when different forms of strategy may be appropriate; and how strategic planning can be useful in formulating strategy and thus in facilitating organisational learning. In doing so, the paper raises some questions for managers who are trying to develop and manage strategy. It is intended at least to help reduce confusion by encouraging managers to think more discriminately about why and how strategy and planning can be important to organisational performance.

What is strategy?

The concept of strategy is a generally accepted one in organisations, but there is an unsettling lack of clarity about what strategy actually is. On the one hand there is an argument that strategy is about 'ends', about objectives, about *what* is to be achieved; on the other, that strategy is about 'means', about processes, about *how* to achieve. The first argument often espouses the view that strategy has more to do with actions to be taken over the long term; the second includes the assertion that strategy has more to do with actions to be taken now. To add to the confusion, there are other arguments made about strategy lying between ends and means, and between long term and now. We are stuck from the onset, it seems, with the question of whether strategy is one thing or another, or whether it can be both or many. It is important to eliminate this ambiguity, if we want to explore how planning can relate to strategy.

STRATEGY IN ORGANISATIONS

Alfred Chandler's study of American industrial enterprise is sometimes cited as the beginning of the scholarly concern with organisational strategy. Chandler quoted Robert Woods, then chairman of Sears, Roebuck and Company: 'Business is like war in one respect, if its grand strategy is correct, any number of tactical errors can be made and yet the enterprise proves successful' and, in time, strategy became a corporate household-word.[1] Chandler defined strategy as the determination of long-term goals, courses of action, and resource allocations. Earlier writers had related the military concept of strategy to the world of business – including the still prolific Peter Drucker.[2] However, Chandler's definition of strategy is important because the confusion about strategy can be neatly represented by the alternative emphases which the definition can be given: strategy as goals, actions, and resources versus strategy as determinator.

Glueck, for example, defines strategy as 'a unified, comprehensive and integrated *plan* designed to assure that basic *objectives* of the enterprise are achieved'.[3] Ohmae, drawing on experiences in Japanese corporations, states that 'strategy is really no more than a plan of action for maximising strength against the forces at work in the business environment'.[4] These definitions of strategy as a plan of actions or tasks are not uncommon in business practice, but they contrast with the definitions of other organisational scholars who see strategy as guidelines for organisational process. 'Strategy is a mediating force between the organisation and its environment', writes Mintzberg.[5] Similarly, Evans advances the idea of 'strategy as a structuring force in the organisation, which defines what are the relevant problems and how and by whom they are to be tackled'.[6] Ansoff gives meaning to the idea of strategy as a guideline or a force by defining strategy as 'a set of decision-making rules for guidance of organisational behaviour'.[7] But what differences are implied by equating either with plans or with guidelines?

PLANS AND GUIDELINES

Plans are comparatively easy to envisage. They are the common outputs of most formal planning exercises. 'A plan . . . is a decision with regard to a course of action'.[8] Plans propose the specific steps of action necessary to achieve organisational objectives, and are 'translatable into needs for people, materials, and money'.[9] These classic definitions of a plan are in keeping with the connotation of strategy as goals, actions and resources. Organisations of many types produce plans which prescribe goals, actions and resource allocations. They label these plans as strategy and often identify strategy as the thing which strategic planning produces.

Mediating forces and guidelines are less easy to define. However, Isenberg's and Kotter's studies of general managers offer help.[10, 11] Both suggest that there are guidelines for corporate behaviour that are often predetermined, if not formally planned, and that they are employed by some managers at least as an implicit business strategy. The guidelines are concerned with regulating organisational process. They are less common as the visable products of strategic planning, but they are based on what should be a central concern of planning: structuring the organisation's activities around important relevant issues. The components of this form of the strategy are all *ways of doing*: gathering information, defining the problem, making networks of problem, looking for implementable programmes, choosing the problem to work on, influencing people – all done in a continuous and incremental manner, in order to structure and sustain the organisation's development around its important issues. This form of strategy comprises what Isenberg defines as *problem management*: to find and define good problems, to map these into a network, and to manage their dynamically shifting priorities.

Now, if we consider the differences between plans and guidelines, it appears that Glueck's and Ohmae's definitions of strategy imply *ends*, while those of Mintzberg and Ansoff connote *means*. This may be the important difference, but there is a more important agreement in their different views. Both views recognise explicitly that what strategy does is to help the organisation manage its environment – either by prescribing actions, or by guiding behaviour. Whether they seek ends or means, whether they espouse plans or guidelines, both see strategy as *management of the interface between the organisation and its environment*. Based on this commonality, a definition of strategy should be able to embrace all forms that deal effectively with the environment. In a very real sense, the form of strategy follows its function. This semantic compromise seems perfectly reasonable in theory, but for the top manager there remains the practical questions: *Which form of strategy does the manager use? Is the interface with the environment managed best by prescribing ends with plans, or by structuring means with guidelines?*

'LIVING' PLANS

One practical answer to these questions has come from blurring the distinction between different forms and regarding plans as guides which help to define problems. This type of plan can be a force for mediating between the organisation and its environment. Quinn's work, for example, illustrates how some top managers design plans to be 'frameworks to guide and provide consistency' for others in the organisation.[12] Their plans are 'living' or 'evergreen'. They teach managers about the long-term future, by exploring contingencies and the effects of alternative ends and of alternative actions; they serve as bases for involving subordinate managers in negotiations about their own short-term goals and tasks. As such, top managers strategic plans become more like organisational guidelines, they become ends to guide means, and thus provide a vehicle for systemising and confirming incremental decisions within the organisation.

For top management, this blurred use of plans seems right. If the organisation's environment *is* the dynamic, turbulent field that Emery and Trist describe[13], then organisations cannot expect to adapt successfully through predetermined actions, the longer-term consequences of which cannot be known with certainty. Instead of prescribed goals and actions, which quickly become obsolete, top managers seek 'a guide and ready calculus' to help cope with environmental uncertainty and change. As turbulence heightens, then, strategy becomes less detailed, more directional and more about *how* and *why* to cope with change than about *what* to do. Living plans may be an answer.

However, citing the turbulent environment of the top manager in order to resolve the differences between detailed plans for action and general guides for behaviour begs two further questions: *First, is a plan which is strictly ends-related ever useful to an organisation? And, second, is the top manager's environment really so turbulent as to always demand means-related strategy?* The questions are interrelated and in trying to answer them we may be able to gain some insight into what planning is for.

The heterogeneous nature of strategy

Organisations do not have *a* strategy, in fact; they have *many* strategies. The multiplicity of strategy is commonly recognised in studies of organisational behaviour. Johnson and Scholes, for example, observe that 'strategies are likely to exist at a number of levels in the organisation': corporate (concerned with what business the organisation is in), competitive (concerned with market position), and operational (concerned with operational functions).[14] Ansoff makes adaptation of the organisation's managerial processes, influence and culture an explicit part of strategy, in keeping with his emphasis on organisational capability and implementation. In effect, Ansoff breaks down competitive strategy into two sets of guidelines: one for developing relationships with the external environment (which he calls 'business strategy') and another for establishing relations and processes within the organisation ('organisational concept').[15] Evans suggests that strategy at any level can have several dimensions, as well: environmental, substantive, organisational, managerial and change (cultural). The role of the strategic manager at any level, he argues, is to coordinate development of these multiple strands while recognising their mutual interdependence and interaction.[16]

We know from practice that a plurality of strategies is commonplace within organisations, both in language and in application. There are different types of guidance and different specificities of plans operating simultaneously at different parts of any organisation. There are corporate missions, which outline the general direction or purpose for all activities of the organisation; there are strategic plans which explore options and provide bases for long-term development and for negotiation inside and outside the organisation; and there are annual programmes which lay out precise short-term targets and criteria for operational control. The pattern is immediately and generally recognisable, so much so that it smacks of the obvious: the answer to the question, 'Which form of strategy does the top manager use?' is both of them – plans and guidelines – and those in between, frequently at the same time. What is not so obvious is what form fits when.

STRATEGY AND TURBULENCE

One simple and common answer to 'Which strategy fits?' has been to refer to time span: as the timing of future action is shortened, strategy is seen as more specific, more a plan than a guideline. As the focus of an organisational unit approaches the operational – that is, as it relates more to operational managers and stable current functions than to top managers and uncertain future markets – strategy takes the form of specific goals, actions and resource allocations. This distinction is similar to that which is often drawn between long-term strategic plans and short-term operational plans. It implies that as we move down the organisation's hierarchy, strategy shifts from general guidelines to specific plans. To use Quinn's analogy, if the top manager's strategy is evergreen, the operational manager's strategy is deciduous.

There is an important lesson in this simplicity, but there is also a danger. The lesson first: generally, as time span lengthens and the particular manager's concern becomes more corporate than functional, uncertainty *is* likely to increase[17] and the strategy required by the manager is more likely to comprise guidance on how to deal with uncertainty than specific targets to be achieved. When the strategy is more about what to do than about ways of doing, when it is more plans than guidelines, it is more likely to risk failure the more turbulent the environment. In that case, the plan may not be a strategy at all.

To illustrate the difference, contrast by example statements from the long-term, *corporate* 'strategies' of two health services organisations. The first organisation, a large health authority in the British National Health Service, prescribes in it's strategic plan a geographic redistribution of acute beds within the region in order to achieve a 'target of 2.0 beds per thousand planning population' by the end of nine years. The second organisation, a combined tertiary care hospital and medical school in North America, identifies its long-term strategy as becoming the 'leader in health care education within its urban environment'. Both strategies provide direction. Both infer environmental linkages. If the environmental of the first organisation shifts uncontrollably, however – say to alter the bases of its planning population – will the strategy of 2.0 beds continue to provide direction or will that specific target become obsolete? If it does become obsolete, then it would be fair to say that the strategic plan does *not* help manage the interface with the environment. It is a response to what was perceived to be the future environment when the plan was struck, but the plan is not strategy. On the other hand, while 'leader' and 'education' may beg definitions of the second organisation, they are more likely to guide continued development even if radical environmental changes should occur. Guidance of organisational behaviour remains in place; the identified important issue of educational leadership gives substance to strategy.

THE FIT OF A STRATEGY

Now, the danger which arises from our simple questions and answers can be demonstrated by trying to judge which of the two examples above is the correct form of strategy. The danger comes from overlooking the fact that the form that strategy takes, and when and where in the organisation that strategy occurs, revolves around a number of factors. Mintzberg identifies at least three: environment, operating systems, and leadership.[18] There are more, including time. Whatever the number, we are not able to judge whether any example of strategy is any more appropriate generally than any other without taking those factors into account as they relate to their individual organisations. Although we might be able to identify what these factors are, they are not simple, their influences vary amongst different organisations, and they are interactive, resulting in different requirements of strategy at different times.

As a result, there can be no general principle about what form strategies should take for all organisations nor about what form strategy should take within one organisation for all time. Strategies cannot be homogeneous. There is no strategy that fits all organisations and times. The long term may not require new guidelines for behaviour if the environment, organisational process, leadership and time do not require it. Conversely, the functional level of the organisation may not find target-based plans helpful if change in its micro-environment is rapid and novel, even though it may be part of a larger more stable organisation.

So, the answer to the lingering questions of whether a plan can ever be a form of strategy which is useful to the top manager and whether the organisations environment always requires guidelines is: 'it depends'. It depends upon what the manager and the organisation need at the time. This is not as flippant nor as simplistic as it sounds.

Pettigrew's analysis of the management of change in a large organisation suggests that finding and clarifying the *content* of any new strategy inevitably entails managing its *context* and *process*.[19] For the manager who is trying to develop strategy, the dependency upon context and process, the influence of environment, organisation, leadership and time, have to be considered in determining what form of strategy will fit. The confusions between guidelines and plans and between means and ends, confusions which can work against management, are often caused by the manager ignoring the question: 'which is needed'? This may be because the manager adopts simple answers and ignores underlying dangers. It also may be because the manager assumes standard planning approaches will help develop strategy without the need for clarifying what form of strategy is required. And that may be because the manager does not think about what planning should be for.

Is planning for learning?

Managers use planning to explore the 'futurity of current decisions'.[20] They use planning to gain an understanding of the changing environment, of the nature of the organisation's business, of its goals, and of what the consequences of its potential actions may be. Planning is regarded essentially as preparing for a

decision, and for the most part, and often despite the consequences, that preparation takes the form of a plan.[21]

Planning can make a significant contribution to the formation
of an organisation's strategy, whether its required form be plan or
guideline. Planning can develop ideas of how actions which managers are about to take will help the organisation to deal with
opportunities and threats in its environment. It can examine
factors around which strategy revolves and explore the ranges of
uncertainty which confront the organisation. As a discipline,
planning has built up some sophisticated and sometimes sensitive
techniques for environmental surveillance, for organisational
analysis and for futures exploration. Textbooks are filled with
these techniques, and some organisations actually use them quite
well in strategy formulation, not simply in producing plans. Shell
International, for example, attributes some of its improved performance to the construction and use of multiple future scenarios
as part of the formation of corporate strategy.[22] Sometimes
organisations do not use planning to help develop strategies, but
Ansoff's longitudinal study of corporate performance demonstrates that 'firms with systematic planning and execution not
only performed significantly better on average, but also were
more predictable in their performance'.[23] So there seem to be
good reasons for managers to use planning; but for what kind of
strategy?

USING PLANNING TO LEARN

Strategy embraces both detailed steps and broad direction, both
specific plans and general guidelines. Confusingly, the vocabulary
of planning seems insistent on defining as 'strategic' any consideration of the long term. But strategy need not be long term. In
some environments, at some times, strategy needs to guide current behaviour and immediate action. Yet despite the changing
demands on strategy, many managers continue to use strategic
planning without questioning or considering to what forms of
strategy their planning is contributing. What those managers fail
to do is to plan the planning. The decision for which those
managers do not prepare, for which they do not plan, is the
decision about what form of strategy is needed.

So what we see in many organisations are formal and established planning processes, which regularly manufacture and
modify formal strategy, without examining whether the form of
strategy on its production line is what the organisation or the
environment demands. What are the results? Long-term action
plans for moving ahead in environments whose turbulence makes

those actions almost instantly inappropriate; grandiose statements to guide behaviour in the face of organisational chaos and incapability; bureaucratised planning systems and schedules which bear little relation to organisational needs; and all other manner of inappropriate strategic products and processes which do not fit.

If the rise of strategic management has taught us anything, it is that strategies must be managed. To do that, managers must have the capacity to continuously learn from the factors around which strategies revolve. Managers must be secure in the understanding that the dynamics of those factors has the potential to make any current strategy obsolete. So strategy and the very processes which help to generate it must be dynamic as well. As the context that influences strategy changes, the content and the form of strategy may have to change as well. That is no bad thing, as long as the manager knows it and acts on the basis of that knowledge. One act can be to use planning to analyse the nature of strategic change.

The focus of many of the analytical techniques and processes of planning can be changed to assess the currency of strategy. Instead of only preparing for decision, planning can be used to implement decision, by surveying, analysing and exploring organisational performance as it relates to current strategies. It can do that by concentrating its analytical capabilities on the factors which influence the formaton of strategy, by assessing the implementation of strategy and by exploring the organisation's potential future performance. In doing so, planning can alert the manager to the needs for change in strategy, not at predetermined intervals, but as environmental turbulence and organisational capability require. With this broader mandate, planning is not only related to strategy formation, it is integral to strategy implementation and to strategy evaluation. It gives rise to an approach which Ansoff calls *strategic learning*, a process in which feedback from strategic moves of the organisation is used to help modify its strategy.[24] Strategy formation and strategy implementation are woven together as interaction processes.

How can the manager use planning to develop the organisation's capacity to learn about the performance of strategy and to employ that learning to develop strategy? First, by making the commitment to monitor and assess strategy, for it can be costly and demanding of management time. But also by adapting and employing planning capabilities of the organistion to examine the interaction of strategy with those factors to which it is meant to respond. Examining the link between environment and organisational process and time demonstrates the point.

ENVIRONMENT AND ORGANISATIONAL PROCESS

Emery and Trist offer a typology of environments ranging from the rather simple, relatively stable to the highly turbulent.[25] An organisation's strategic response should be geared to a reading of environmental variations within that range. Ansoff suggests a number of characteristics which merit ongoing analysis, including predictability and frequency of change, novelty, technological intensity, and societal pressure, amongst others. As the level of turbulence shifts, organisational behaviour requires change. He suggests, for example, that as the environment moves from relative stability to high creativity, organisational process must move beyond structural responsibilities to informal task forces and teams or networks which cross organisational lines. Organisational processes must change.[26]

Hurst's account of events at Hugh Russel Inc, a large public steel company in Canada, shows that as environmental crisis mounts that is exactly what happens: 'hard box solutions' give way to 'soft bubble resolution' if the organisation is to survive. When an environment of rapid growth shifted quickly to threaten Russelsteel's survival, organisational arrangements which fit a growth market proved to be cumbersome, expensive, and impotent. The logical framework of hard (organistional chart) boxes limited innovatory response. Problem management required issue-related networks or soft bubbles of managers which broke through hierarchical accountabilities and internal competitiveness.[27]

As well as being an integral component of strategy, organisational process can influence what strategy should be. Unfortunately, the relationship sometimes can be more parasitic than symbiotic. Mintzberg's examination of organisational process and performance shows that when change is required some organisations 'maintain internal consistency at the expense of a gradually worsening fit with the environment'.[28] Quinn's work suggests that this misfit manifests itself as a lack of innovation. Top management isolation, excessive rationalisation (particularly within the planning process), excessive bureaucracy, and inflexible reward and control systems are among the constraints. If these constraints are damaging performance, Quinn argues, a new 'strategy for innovation' is required, which may include more complex portfolio planning, an opportunity orientation and perhaps even restructuring.[29] These kinds of constraints need monitoring, if strategy is to respond.

There is a need in organisations for top management to be able to identify when environmental conditions require internal adaptation, when boxes or bubbles become more appropriate, when innovation is stifled. Survey, analysis and exploration of the environment – activities central to strategic planning – can make important contributions to organisational success by testing internal capabilities against external threats and opportunities, and by helping managers to learn when strategy needs change.

ENVIRONMENT AND TIME

The life-cycle of change is important to a strategy's usefulness. Pettigrew's study shows that strategic change does not necessarily occur in a gradual evolutionary manner, but can entail stages of rapid development followed by long periods of relative continuity, stabilisation and adjustment.[30] This organisational phenomenon has its parallels in the science of natural evolution, where theories of gradualism are giving way to an understanding of the episodic nature of evolutionary change – the theory of 'punctuated equilibrium', popularised by Stephen Jay Gould.[31] As the cycle of times moves on, from lengthy periods of continuity to sudden periods of rapid change, the strategy (or, in evolutionary terms, the diversity of the species) needed to cope with the new environment must change as well. When stability returns, strategy again assumes the direction of stabilisation and adjustment.

As the cycle or organisational change moves on, the influences of other factors on strategy formation become more or less important. Bartlett's study of EMI and its entry into the diagnostic imaging business is a clear illustration: 'Although the decisions involved in the early stages . . . can be made centrally, as the cycle progresses decisions increasingly must be made in response to market developments.' EMI's entry strategy failed in the mature stages of the business cycle because it did not cope with the complex customer, technological and competitive change which previously were not so important. Organisational and managerial strategies did not adjust, largely because EMI did not develop a capacity 'to sense, analyse, decide, and respond' to complex change.[32] The absence of a planning-learning capability contributed largely to EMI's eventual failure.

The manager as strategic learner

Linking ideas about what strategy is, about when different forms of strategy are important, and about the usefulness of strategic planning in organisations gives rise to the notion of the top manager as strategic learner. The top manager is not merely the generator of strategy, nor merely its implementor, but takes on the added burdens of organisational uncertainty, error and evolution. As a consequence, strategy formation is used to modify current strategy. Argyris and Schön give the name 'double-loop learning' to the diagnostic and adaptive processes which 'resolve incompatible organisational norms by setting new priorities and weighing of norms, or by restructuring the norms themselves together with associated strategies and assumptions.[33]

Within this context, to separate strategic planning from strategy implementation or from the managment of change is to make 'the manager as strategist' an empty concept. The analytical, developmental, and explorative tools of planning can provide the manager with information and signals that are essential to the management of the organisation's strategies. To employ those tools, the manager needs to develop a clear sense of how strategies relate organisational dynamic to environmental turbulence.

Planning, implementation and change are not discrete phases of that organisational dynamic. They all contribute to organisational learning and at the same time they interact to provide the manager with a framework for achieving success. In an important sense, as components of management, they require strategies themselves. For strategic planning, then, analytical, developmental and explorative processes must be able to continuously and incrementally adapt and change. For the manager as strategist, strategic planning must be planned.

References

1 Chandler A J. 1962: Strategy and structures: chapters in the history of the American industrial enterprise. Cambridge, MA, MIT Press: p 235.
2 Drucker P. The practice of management, New York, Harper & Brothers, 1954.
3 Glueck W. Business policy, strategy formation and management action (2nd edition). New York, McGraw-Hill, 1976: p 3.
4 Ohmae K. The mind of the strategist. London, Penguin, 1983: p 248.
5 Mintzberg H. The structuring of organisations. Englewood Cliffs, NJ, Prentice Hall, 1979: p 25.
6 See Evans, T. Strategic response to environmental turbulence (chapter 1 of this book, p 18).
7 Ansoff H I. Implanting strategic management. London, Prentice Hall, 1984: p 31.
8 Banfield E C. Ends and means in planning. International Social Science Journal, 11, 3, 1959. Reprinted in Faludi A. A reader in planning theory. Oxford, Pergamon, 1973: p 140.
9 Koontz H and O'Donnell C. Management: a systems and contingency analysis of management functions, 5th edition. New York, McGraw-Hill, 1976: p 263.

10 Isenberg D J. How senior managers think. Harvard Business Review, Nov-Dec, 1984.
11 Kotter J P. The general manager. New York, The Free Press, 1982.
12 Quinn J B. Managing strategies incrementally. Omega, International Journal of Management Science, 10, 6, 1982: p 617.
13 Emery F E and Trist E L. The casual texture of organisational environment. Human Relations, 18, 1965.
14 Johnson G and Scholes K. Exploring corporate strategy. London, Prentice Hall, 1984: p 9.
15 See 7: p 31.
16 See 6.
17 Mintzberg H. Patterns in strategy formation. Management Science, 24, 9, 1978.
18 See 17.
19 Pettigrew A M. The awakening giant: continuity and change in Imperial Chemical Industries. Oxford, Basil Blackwell, 1985: p 439.
20 Steiner G A and Miner J B. Management policy and strategy. New York, Macmillan, 1982: p 94.
21 Woodward T M. Should corporate planners plan? Address to the Business Week Corporate Planning Conference, April, 1981.
22 Schoemaker P. The scenario approach to planning. Address to a conference of the Society for Strategic and Long Range Planning and the Operational Research Society, London, February, 1984.
23 See 7: p 195.
24 See 7: p 485.
25 See 13.
26 Ansoff H I. Strategic management. London, Macmillan, 1979.
27 Hurst D K. Of boxes, bubbles, and effective management. Harvard Business Review, May–June, 1982.
28 Mintzberg H. Organisation design: fashion or fit? Harvard Business Review, Jan–Feb, 1981.
29 Quinn J B. Managing innovation: controlled chaos. Harvard Business Review, May–June, 1985.
30 See 19. •
31 Gould S J. The panda's thumb. London, Pelican, 1980.
32 Bartlett C A. EMI and the CT scanner. Harvard Business School Case, Cambridge, MA, Harvard College, 1983.
33 Argyris C and Schön D A. Organisational learning: a theory of action perspective. Reading, MA, Addison-Wesley, 1978: p 24.

6

Strategic planning in a political context: the case of AIDS

A S MACPHERSON

At first glance, the problem of AIDS may seem ill-suited for a seminar on strategic planning. On more careful examination, however, the analysis of this modern plague can be undertaken productively in the strategic planning framework. It is a typical example of the need for the organization to build in the ability to change rapidly in response to a changing environment. In this paper, I outline the biology and epidemiology of the disease, look at societal trends in terms of both external constraints and the relatively few opportunities that exist, look at the stakeholders, suggest a desired direction and outline some actions we took in the city of Toronto.

AIDS is an infectious disease which first came to the attention of western medicine about 1979. The inability of the body to resist infection or prevent the spread of some types of rare cancers led to the name Acquired Immune Deficiency Syndrome abbreviated to AIDS. Throughout this paper, this late stage of the disease will be referred to as 'classical AIDS'. Other stages of the disease will be referred to as 'AIDS infection'. 'AIDS' unqualified refers to any stage of the disease. These distinctions are necessary because much confusion has arisen from imprecise use of the term. In order to understand the current situation, I will discuss first what little is known about the natural history of the disease and consider the epidemiology.

Natural history of AIDS

The causative agent in AIDS is believed to be the HTLV III/ LAV* virus. Whether this virus alone is capable of causing AIDS, or whether other circumstances are required, is not at all clear. Current thinking is that for the disease to progress the human T lymphocytes must be activated. This is most usually done by another viral infection such as infectious mononucleosis or cytomegalo virus. In any case, it is now believed that 90–95 per cent of those infected with the virus will not develop clinical

*HTLV III means human T lymphocyte virus as the American co-discoverers named it. LAV means lymphadenopathy associated virus so named by the French co-discoverers.

illness. Whether or not this group can transmit the virus to others is not yet known. A proportion of those infected may develop the so called AIDS-related complex (ARC). AIDS-related complex is characterized by fatigue and swollen lymph glands. In some persons, ARC may be the only outcome of an HTLV III infection. In other cases, the infection may proceed, eventually overwhelming the immune system and producing the classical symptomatology of AIDS. An important recent observation is the effect of the virus on the central nervous system. This may produce behavioural change.

Who can infect others? It is important to stress that AIDS is *not* a highly infectious disease. To date, despite intimate contact, only two health workers not in high risk groups have been known to develop AIDS. Both these individuals accidentally stuck themselves with needles. AIDS transmission from sibling to sibling has not been described. In only one documented case has a parent acquired AIDS from a child. It is therefore not reasonable to institute quarantine style precautions for AIDS patients in general. Certain practices associated with very close personal contact, such as sharing the same toothbrush (because of blood, not saliva) or the same razor are not indicated.

There are only four known ways to contract AIDS. The first, and by far the most important, is sexual transmission, particularly anal intercourse. This is probably because the anal wall is much thinner, tears more easily, and is more easily penetrated than the vaginal wall by the virus. A recent case report of five women who became HTLV positive following artificial insemination is instructive. It illustrates the ability of semen to transmit the disease. Despite unprotected intercourse, however, none of the husbands had become HTLV antibody positive.

The second known route of infection is by infected needle. This has been a relatively common route of infection in the US, but is much less common in Canada. Infection by needle may be by deliberate use of the needle as in drug users or accidental as with health care workers.

The third method of transmission is by blood transfusion. Obviously users of pooled blood products such as haemophiliacs are at much higher risk, although infection transmitted by transfusion, in the course of usual surgical procedures, is described. Finally, transmission from mother to child, usually transplacentally, is known to occur.

The absence of documentation for other routes does not mean they do not exist. It simply means that they must be sufficiently rare not to have turned up as yet in the course of this epidemic and therefore are of substantially less importance in considering control strategies.

DIAGNOSIS

HTLV III virus in an antigen. That is, in the early stages of the disease, the human body attempts to neutralize the virus by producing antibodies. It is important to note that the body produces more than one kind of antibody. Some antibodies confer immunity. The AIDS antibody we now measure is *not* an indication of immunity. These antibodies can be detected by several techniques, most commonly by a method called Elisa. This indicates that the virus is there now but does not give information about the state of the disease. (This statement illustrates the difficulty and uncertainty in making statements about AIDS. Since the initial preparation of this paper, a consensus has developed that HTLV III/LAV antibody-positive individuals must be considered as having the virus present and therefore potentially infective.) Nevertheless, the presence of this antibody permits us to detect individuals who have been exposed and who therefore may be at risk of passing on the virus. These individuals can then be counselled about habits and lifestyle.

The use of a diagnostic screening test is not without problems. All diagnostic tests have false positive and false negative results. The extent to which a test demonstrates these results is known as sensitivity and specificity. Sensitivity is the proportion of true positives that are detected by the test and specificity is the proportion of true negatives that are called negative by the test. Commercial Elisa test kits available now for the diagnosis of the HTLV III antibody are reported to have a sensitivity of 95 per cent and a specificity of up to 99.8 per cent.

The interpretation of results of a diagnostic or screening test depends on the prevalence of the condition to be detected. At this point we will only report that in a high prevalence population (40 per cent infected), a single positive Elisa test means the person is truly infected 99.7 per cent of the time. In a hypothetical general population (1 in 10,000 infected), this positive predictive value will be 4.5 per cent. In either case the person with a positive test is 200 times more likely to have the disease than a person with a negative test. This excursion into statistics is necessary to understand the controversy about screening for AIDS infection. In practice, a single Elisa test is always repeated for confirmation and verified by a different test. This results in a very low false positive rate. Recently, the American Medical Association came up with two distinct sets of recommendations, depending on whether the individuals screened belonged to a high risk or a low risk group. These figures show why. Actually, the screening tests for AIDS perform extremely well and are well within the levels of sensitivity and specificity for most tests.

In summary, we have as yet a rather incomplete knowledge of the natural history of AIDS virus infection and its various ramifications. We do have a diagnostic test but its applicability for general population screening is still the subject of some controversy. The question of who to screen, as well as how to deal with the positives, has not been fully thought through.

The impact on public health

It is important to recognize that this new fatal disease is a major and serious public health problem. In the City of Toronto in 1985, AIDS was the second commonest cause of death in males aged 30–39. AIDS is predicted to be the commonest cause of death in males of this age group in Ontario in 1986. Although I do not subscribe to the doomsday scenarios, a number of highly responsible microbiologists have called AIDS the wost plague since the 15th century. The outcome for those who progress to the classical AIDS syndrome now is fatal, but the years ahead will give us a beter understanding of the epidemiology in terms of the likelihood of an HTLV III/LAV infection progressing to classical AIDS. We may also learn a great deal more about in which phases of the disease it is transmissible.

While the disease is new, this kind of health problem is not. In the early years of this century, syphilis and tuberculosis were major causes of disability and death. Physicians and nurses worked in fever hospitals where they daily exposed themselves to the risk of infection for which there was no treatment. As we advanced into the 20th century and the germ theory of disease gained wide acceptance, the response was substantially different from the response of AIDS today. There was mandatory reporting of infectious disease, vigorous follow-up of contacts, a very wide screening net. In the case of syphilis, the Wasserman test was considerably less specific than the Elisa test for AIDS. Nevertheless, Wasserman tests were obligatory in many states and provinces to obtain a marriage certificate. Pre-employment physicals and hospital admissions were always accompanied by a Wasserman, as was entry into the armed forces. The possibility of quarantine also existed – and indeed exists to this day – with specialized hospitals established for the treatment of contagious disease.

Community health management

AIDS has evoked again many of the primitive fears that accompanied earlier infectious diseases. A priority in the community health management of AIDS has been to fight the fear of AIDS. However, this objective should not conflict with the mission of public health which is to prevent the spread of AIDS.

Today's society places higher importance on individual rights than in the past. Some public health intervention, particularly the strong powers of detention and quarantine, are based on the now less popular utilitarian approach to jurisprudence. The individual has the right to privacy and freedom from unnecessary harassment. The individual does not have the right to infect others with a potentially fatal disease.

Against this background, local health authorities in high risk areas around the world struggle to maintain credibility with the public, retain the confidence of high risk groups, balance individual and collective rights and attempt to reduce the spread of AIDS. The high public profile, the emotional impact of this disease on those affected, the uncertainty about its management, and the variety of fears require careful analysis of the roles, attitudes and position of the stakeholders. It is also essential for the organization to build in flexibility and responsiveness to change in order to maintain its mission and to control the disease. In what follows, I will become increasingly specific about the experience of one local health authority in Toronto, Ontario, in developing a strategy to deal with the problems of AIDS. Our experience is likely to be not too different from a dozen other cities in the western world.

THE ENVIRONMENT

In doing an environmental scan, we have found that the following elements need to be taken into account:

1 The homosexual community – This community has been at the highest risk for the development of AIDS and was among the first group to become seriously concerned. As a result, they acquired an expertise long before most public health officials or government were interested. They have claimed that the public's relative lack of interest in AIDS, until quite recently, is the result of homophobia. The opposite may be true, our modern concern for civil rights having inhibited us from imposing sanctions on vulnerable groups easily subject to discrimination. Today, gay groups are well organized in most communities where there are sufficient numbers of AIDS cases. They perform a very useful

self-help function, while at the same time, providing substantial policy input to governments. The role of these groups is difficult since, on one hand, they do not wish to unduly alarm or foster the 'new leper' attitude. On the other hand, they wish to draw attention to the seriousness of the situation, and to attract government funding.

2 The general public – The public is not homogeneous; it varies from extreme emotional reaction towards homosexuals, homosexual activity and AIDS to strong compassion for the plight of the classical AIDS patient. Some elements of the general public seem to be fulfilling the gay groups' worst fears. They express a widespread fear and anxiety about AIDS in the community. Fortunately in Canada these elements comprise a relatively small proportion of the population. A more substantial group of the public sense an express distaste and disapproval of the homosexual lifestyle. Many found the explicit language and description necessary to reach the high risk population offensive. Perhaps the largest group of all are the people who have a basic inclination to be compassionate, but who are ill-informed and to some extent distrustful of the meagre information available. Initially there was not a great deal they could be told about AIDS with authority, and this aggravated their problem. Finally, a minority of the public were initially compassionate, made themselves well-informed and became valuable allies in the development of self-help.

3 Public Health – The public health community was slow to get involved. Until quite recently in Ontario, AIDS policy was being developed by one provincial epidemiologist working part-time on the problem and, apparently, by the Minister's political staff. In Canada, advisory committees have tended to be composed of basic scientists and clinicians, not public health professionals. Because of concerns about backlash, there has been apparent reluctance on the part of the public health community to play an aggressive role in the control of this disease. While it has usually been the public health response to err on the side of safety when there is reasonable and probable cause to do so, this has not happened with AIDS.

4 Government – In the absence of firm public health direction, government has been guided largely by political considerations. Perhaps the most dramatic example of this occurred in Ontario where the Minister of Health partially rescinded, apparently on political advice, regulations that had just been proclaimed con-

cerning the reportability of AIDS. His action had the effect of making it virtually impossible to track the spread of the disease to new risk groups. It took six months to get this position reversed.

5 Health professionals – The role of health professionals has been extremely mixed. Significant numbers of physicians, dentists and nurses have appeared to have forgotten the longstanding commitment of their professions to the care of those with infectious disease. Membership in medicine or nursing implies a willingness to expose oneself to risk and indeed many have done so willingly. Nevertheless, the special needs of the health care worker groups have not been adequately considered by public health or hospital administrations or perhaps even by gay rights groups.

6 Educational authorities – In the spring of 1985, the school system in New York City erupted as parents refused to send their children to school with children with AIDS. In Toronto, officials became concerned that a similar situation could occur. Teachers' unions sought further information. School trustees were approached by anxious parents and school administrators sought explicit procedures to deal with children with AIDS.

7 Red Cross – The Red Cross is a stakeholder because prior to the development of the screening test blood and blood products were a major concern in the threat of AIDS. The advent of a screening test for AIDS posed many problems for the Red Cross. The Red Cross must maintain the supply of transfusable blood both in quantity and quality. They have a strong tradition of confidentiality for their donors. They were reluctant to report positive tests and ill equipped to do the follow-up themselves.

BUILDING RESPONSIVENESS WITH THE ORGANIZATION

In Ontario, health units are local public health authorities. They are governed by boards of health composed of politicians and politically active lay persons. Board meetings are public and attended by the media. In Toronto, the Board of Health regularly hears deputations from concerned citizens. These practices impose responsiveness on the staff.

This formal input is not enough in developing a plan to deal with the AIDS epidemic. We found that we must reach out and maintain regular contact with all the stakeholders in the en vironment. To combat fear of AIDS, two senior managers were appointed to OPEDA – the Ontario Public Education Panel on AIDS. This group was sponsored and funded by the Minister of Health to produce educational material about AIDS.

Membership included the Red Cross, the AIDS Committee of Toronto (a self-help group), representatives of nursing, and a clinician. We also requested and were granted observer status on the Provincial Advisory Committee on AIDS

We formed a working group with the school authorities in Toronto, emphasizing that there were at that time no cases of transmission of AIDS between parent and child, except at birth, or between siblings, even in the intimate contact of family life. Since there is no evidence that AIDS is transmitted by usual social contact, there is no need to inform school authorities about cases and there is no need to bar such children from school for the protection of others. In each case, the health authorities will evaluate the child. To increase the amount of information available, we circulated a joint statement to school staff, we made senior department staff available to talk with parents and teachers, and I briefed an elected school trustee from each of the two boards we serve.

When the public storm broke, it was over a teacher who was alleged to have died from AIDS. We were prepared, and able to present a consistent, scientifically accurate and therefore reassuring message to public, parents and teachers.

We formed a committee to set the ground rules for follow-up of individuals reported positive for HTLV III/LAV antibody. We included in the group, a representative of the AIDS Committee of Toronto and a physician who was well known for his civic libertarian views on screening for AIDS.

A senior staff member with a haemophiliac child became extremely active with respect to the AIDS issue in haemophiliacs. He represented the haemophiliac society on a number of local and national groups dealing with AIDS problems. This brought not only the perspective of the at risk population, but the public health perspective as well.

Fear of AIDS is now diminishing, spread of the disease is slowing, in our community at least. The turbulence of 1984 and 1985 seriously challenged public health in North America. We were slow to realize the changing and unstable social and ethical environment. This unusual example demonstrates the usefulness of the strategic planning approach in an area other than resource allocation and priority setting.

7

Strategic planning in a function at national level

R W DEARDEN

This paper presents a case study in strategic management in an unusual combination of circumstances. The case entails the production of a strategic plan for the new National Health Service Training Authority for England and Wales.

The functions of the Authority (NHSTA) are described, along with the service environment in which the strategic plan was to be put into context. There then follows an outline of the process followed to articulate a national training strategy and an indication of its main values and priorities.

Finally some observations are offered on features of strategic management in a function at national level.

The NHSTA

At issue was the development and establishment of a national training strategy for the health service in England and Wales. There had never been any such strategy, although government departments had been involved in health service corporate planning since at least 1974 and some training functions had been carried out by central government departments until 1983. At that time, a new body – the NHSTA – was created to take responsibility for what had previously been central government responsibilities in training, but within the NHS.

The NHSTA was created as a special health authority and formally took over its responsibilities in October, 1983; it acquired its first budget in April, 1984. The functions of the Authority are quite widely defined to include identification of NHS training needs, formulation of policies and standards, and provision and review of training programmes. In addition to training in a very broad sense, they include some employment practices and research. The Authority is not responsible for basic professional education (for example, of doctors or nurses) but otherwise is involved with a full range of educational and training activities including continuing education, skills training, management education and development, involving all types of NHS personnel from ambulance men and cooks through to doctors, nurses, general managers and members of health authorities.

The environment

Obviously the major goings on in the NHS generally, and other issues in the Training Authority specifically, had significant impacts on the development and content of a national training strategy. To indicate the extent of these influences, the main external and internal features of the environment are described below:

1 The creation of a new Training Authority and devolution of responsibilities from Department of Health and Social Security (DHSS) to the NHS was widely welcomed in the health service. This got the Authority off to a good start. The membership of the Authority is drawn from members and managers of health authorities in England and Wales. From the beginning there was a willingness and an eagerness to support the notion that there should be a national training strategy. At the same time, this has led to high expectations with little knowledge or interest in the constraining factors in the other parts of the Authority's environment.

2 Following the recommendations of a Management Inquiry Report on the NHS (the Griffiths report), government policy is to change fundamentally the nature and role of management in the health service. A key feature of this change is to move from the historical pattern of functional and consensus management to a pattern of general management more recognisable in other services and industries and perhaps in other nations' health services. This has meant much turbulance and change in health authorities, creating a very anxious and uncertain climate for other major health issues. At the same time, it immediately thrust the Training Authority into the limelight as having a key role in supporting these changes and producing matching radical development in the management education system.

3 The health service as a whole continued to grapple with successive manpower cuts and uneven reductions in spending power, whilst coping with national and local priority imperatives, demographic change and medical technological advance. Whilst in some ways this environment forces change, in other ways it makes change more difficult by contributing to a more hostile environment for anybody with a developmental message.

4 Part of the implementation of the Griffiths report included the establishment of a National Board for the NHS, with an industrial manager brought in as Chairman. This resulted in renewed

attention to issues of accountability. The National Board and its Chairman have clear responsibilities for national level management of the NHS, with high expectations placed upon them both by Ministers and by the NHS. At the same time, the formal position is that regional health authority chairmen continue to be accountable to ministers and not to the Chairman of the National Board, and their regional general managers are accountable to the regional authorities and not to the National Board. Whilst considerable effort has gone into clarifying roles and relationships informally, this situation has not been formally clarified or resolved in practice. The position of the NHSTA is a complicated microcosm of this tension. The Authority has to be seen as delivering the goods by both the NHS and the Management Board or it will lose support in practical terms. The NHS is a large, diffuse and inconsistent organism. In political and practical terms, this aspect of accountability has so far amounted to seeking and ensuring the support of regional chairmen, advised by their general managers, for Training Authority major strategies and initiatives. At the same time, trade unions that historically have been heavily represented in the national level training machinery are keen to maintain their influence. This is partly achieved by two trade union members of the Authority. Accordingly it would be difficult to make progress on major change if this were felt to threaten important trade union interests – although in practice this has rarely been a problem so far.

5 Within the Training Authority itself, a number of factors influenced the short-term action agenda comprising part of the internal environment for strategic planning. These internal factors included staffing, office location and inherited programmes and systems.

The headquarters staffing of the Authority was from the beginning and until well into 1985 the inherited staff from DHSS on a seconded basis. I joined the Authority in March 1984 as Chief Executive and for the following eight months was the only permanent substantive member of staff. The difficulties that posed are obvious. At the same time it was urgent to define a new organisational philosophy related to staffing structure and to recruit around 50 new posts from the most junior to the most senior on a very short timescale.

Over that same timescale, the decision was made and implemented to relocate from London to Bristol. Whilst this is of both immediate and long-term benefit, particularly in financial and recruitment terms, the additional workload and turbulence was competing for time and energy.

Finally, the Authority inherited many things from government training departments. These included a range of programmes which had never been planned or subjected to any coherent policy but which self-avowedly had been incremental responses to pressures of the day. This meant that it was easy to get agreement that there should be an overall plan and programmes shaped to a planned view of priorities, but there was also a heavy investment of resources and energy in the existent, each individual part being someone's baby and beloved of a vested interest.

The inherited administrative machinery and infrastructure that gave rise to previous programmes was both excessive and inappropriate. On the one hand, the machinery tended simply to represent the large number of health service vested interests which resulted in over 50 committees of various kinds. Almost all of these had to be abolished on the same timescale, the efforts again competing for time and energy. A significant proportion of the infrastructure rested upon designated national education centres funded by a historical incremental block grant, with little idea of objectives, workload and accountability. Again this had to be changed on the same timescale. However, because the functions had previously been carried out by one small part of a very large government department, there were precious few, if any, inherited budget systems or procedures appropriate to an accountable separate organisation established as a special health authority. So, there was a need for basic housekeeping, which it was important to get right and to get done on the same timescale.

Process

What is the right way to stimulate thought and to develop, establish and implement strategies in a function at national level, with a new body operating in the environment described above? The answers are not obvious, although there are some obvious 'don'ts'. The two extremes to be avoided, both well established in the British NHS, are on the one hand the top down bureaucratic statement 'here it is – get out of that' and, on the other hand, protracted repetitious consultation resulting in wishy-washy well intentioned manifestos. Because of the relatively few useful measures of productivity and even fewer measures of effectiveness, it is easier than usual to make motherhood and apple pie statements in training matters. A further complication is that working at national level is like working in a goldfish bowl. There is no shortage of examples of defunct national bodies which became extinct at least partly by not getting right the process of having good ideas, communicating them well, being responsive to the various constituencies and putting them into practice.

In the event the following process was followed:

Spring 1984 – publication of *Investing in People – The Future*, being partly an explanation of the Authority's role, function and intentions, but mainly a series of structured questions addressed primarily to the NHS on what changes were sought and major issues of substance to be identified.

Summer/Autumn 1984 – discussion papers, informal ad hoc seminars, some policy statements, commitment to Ministers to produce a draft strategic plan by July 1985 and a substantive strategic plan by the following November.

Winter/Spring 1985 – more informal discussion papers, seminars, and so on.

Spring 1985 – NHSTA approves publication of consultation document *An Outline for a National Training Strategy*. Building on previous steps this document outlines emerging policies, indicates possible future directions and defines unresolved issues; response at all levels on each part is sought.

Spring/Summer 1985 – informal discussions, teach-ins, and so on. Supportive, positive and in parts sophisticated response to consultation document.

July 1985 – NHSTA agrees draft strategic plan to be submitted to DHSS and National Board. Further work and consideration of continuing consultation responses.

September 1985 – NHSTA further considers responses and latest work finalises substantive strategic plan.

Autumn 1985 – Substantive strategic plan submitted to DHSS and National Board and made available to NHS training infrastructure. Full strategy available on request, short 'popular' version published widely throughout the service.

Content

The outcome of all this is a document of approximately 30 pages. It has the obligatory mission statement, describes a fairly short list of priorities and makes position statements on the main subject areas, notably management education and development, professional and occupational training and training methodology.

With regard to the priorities and statements of intent the attempt was made to make definite statements with which it is possible to disagree and where feasible to draw out the entailed practical implications. The extent to which we have succeeded in this will be determined by wiser heads. An extract from the strategic plan, comprising its summary, is quoted in full:

Time is a scarce commodity and you may not be able to read all of the Outline Strategy. Please use the summary on the following pages to get an impression of the total document before referring to the section or sections which are of particular interest. The minimum that will give you a coherent impression of the total document is the summary and section one – the introduction.

Summary

This document sets out the NHSTA's outline for a national training strategy. At this stage, the views expressed in the document are initial guidelines rather than fixed proposals and we will welcome any suggestions as to ways in which our proposals could be enhanced.

Our outline is split into seven sections and an appendix appears at the end of the document. Briefly, these sections deal with:

1 Introduction

In our introduction we set out what we at the NHSTA believe our mission to be and we give some of the reasons why a national training strategy is needed. We introduce those training areas which we believe warant the highest priorities and set out our philosophy in some detail.

2 Management development

Management development is one of the areas we select for priority treatment. In this section we set out the need to develop suitable candidates for management careers and discuss how they should best be developed. We describe our major review of all NHS management education, training and development. We highlight the fact that different approaches will be needed when training doctors as opposed to other NHS managers and suggest what these might be. Consideration is also given as to how we could deal with management budgeting and the introduction of information technology.

3 Professional and occupational training

We highlight five main areas where we feel we should get involved. These include: training for people new to a post;

meeting service wide training needs such as developing 'customer relations' skills; providing up-date training when the skill and knowledge requirements of a job change; retraining staff for new work roles when the purpose and boundaries of the job change; redeployment training. Consideration is also given in this section to the way in which the NHSTA can help when the pattern of health service provision changes, for example alterations in the provision of care for the elderly. Finally, we outline what we consider our priorities to be.

4 Training methodology and technology

We believe that it is possible to provide more, better trained individuals to the Health Service by optimising our training resources. In this section we outline some of the processes we would use to deliver training and define the need for trainers in a consultant rather than instrumental role. We introduce our proposal to transform the existing Training Aids Centre into a new training media and media skill development unit and discuss the use of various new training methods, techniques and technologies.

5 Performance review

We are keen for there to be a system which indicates how our training activities and those of others are performing. In this section we give bases on which performance could be judged and suggest ways in which our efforts could be analysed and assessed.

6 Funding policy

We propose that as a general principle mainstream programmes should not be 'free' but charged at an 'at cost' figure. The funding policy section sets out the reasons for this proposal and gives examples of cases which might be considered to be exceptions to the rule.

7 Role and relationships

The NHSTA's work can only be effective if it can co-operate successfully with others. This section outlines the way in which we see our relationship with the NHS, the DHSS and the outside training world. We also explain the roles of National Education Centres and National Health Service Training Authority Centes.

Concluding observations

This case study is presented not from the point of view of something done well for the edification of others, but rather to share a learning experience from someone with some experience of strategic management and planning, struggling with new issues, context, dimensions and environment. We would all do it better next time. In that context the following personal observations are offered.

1 Strategic planning and management is never easy, but is harder in a context of multiple or ambiguous lines of accountability. The position of the NHSTA in this regard is described above. On reflection I feel that the difference between national and local strategic management in this regard is one of degree, rather than kind. All health managers, whatever their formal positions, have to relate to a range of different kinds of constituencies, which need to be minimally satisfied. Perhaps this is intrinsic to all times and places in the planning and provision of such an important and personal service as health.

In Britain, the district general manager's accountability to the health authority and the chairman in particular may be clear, but it is also clear that he or she could well be in trouble if a number of constituencies (and therefore 'accountabilities') are not satisfied. The regional general manager can be expected to have a significant impact on whether the district general manager is deemed to be successful. It should be noted that both the regional general manager and the chairmen can change at fairly short notice and that the picture will become more complex with the advent of performance related pay. Consultant medical staff, consumer and political organisations and trade unions are all examples of other factors which at various times and places have the capacity to materially affect the judgment as to whether a general manager and a strategy have been successful. In America and Australia, for example, the fluctuations of a market health economy or radical change of the rules by the Federal government similarly can override other perceptions of accountability and performance.

2 Everybody wants a new bus service provided the stop isn't exactly outside my house. Everybody wants national priorities, provided it does not take away anything I have got and preferably gives me some more. Readers will feel that this observation is true of strategic managment in any context. My observation having moved from district management to national level, is that the force and dimensions of this are much greater at national level. This is amplified by the goldfish bowl effect.

3 Another factor in strategic management in any context, but again one that I feel is amplified at national level, is the enhanced subtlety of striking the right balance between sensitivity to the constituencies and getting something done. Given a large canvas including a large number and variety of constituencies on any one issue at any one time, there will be some who demand the status quo, some requiring radical change, some who don't give a damn, and yet others who are downright contrasuggestible. This range of responses can be found even within one constituency – for example, health authority members. It is easy to see why strategic managers at national level become seduced into one of three postures according to temperament: insensitive, dynamic 'push it through'; interminable inconclusive sensitivity; and cynical token consultation playing off one constituency against another. Given the importance of getting the balance right, I conclude that it is important at the personal level to have confidential and trusted points of reference – organisational wise uncles or whatever – as a source of feedback and therapy.

Organisationally to strike this sort of balance it is highly desirable and perhaps essential to develop a learning culture as part of how that organisation works. As a new organisation, the NHSTA has in place some mechanisms and processes for securing feedback information and is establishing more. Work has begun on the more complex and subtle process of what and how we learn from that information. Learning is often accelerated where uncertainty is tolerated, conflict is managed and mistakes are tolerated. NHSTA has certainly had its share of uncertainty, conflict and mistakes and internally the learning is very fast. This is helped by staff sharing a common vested interest in NHS staff development, rather than the incompatible vested interests frequently found in heterogeneous health authorities. It is also helped by the leading staff themselves being professional educational and training staff and therefore attuned to the need for optimising the use of learning opportunities. Establishing a learning-loop with the outside world is more difficult as the NHS is more prone to rush onto the next crisis rather than learn from the last one and to move away from mistakes as rapidly as possible, rather than spend time learning from them.

4 Successful strategic management must by definition be breaking new ground, at least some of the time. This case study is about breaking a lot of new ground in a short timescale with few signposts or maps. However much thought is given to the

objectives and the plan, however much sensitivity there is to constituencies and however textbook perfect the strategic manager or management is, there comes a point where knowledge, advice and authority all run out and someone has to say, 'let's do this'. So strategic management not only implies the courage to break new ground, but also the willingness to make mistakes (often enough said) and also the ability to live with them (more difficult).

5 'Only the Health Service thinks plans are for implementing' (G Best, Fellow, King's Fund College). Feeling committed to a strategic plan which represents the investment of so much personal time and energy naturally leads to wanting to shape the world to that plan, which in a stratified bureaucracy means that the planning system easily becomes an obstacle to action rather than its vehicle. 'The plan' determines timetables and prevents seizing opportunities or changing the game to meet changing circumstances. It is crucial to have a plan if we are to avoid creeping incrementalism, or bouncing from pillar to post; it is equally crucial that we do not become servants to the plan rather than its master. At the same time, health service managers, certainly those in the NHS, will be familiar with the phenomenon of the yawning gap between strategic intent and operational delivery. Even a casual reading of the newspapers suggests this is not an unknown phenomenon in purposive dynamic private enterprise. In this sense, production of the strategic plan is the easy bit. An effective implementation plan and process has to come next. Recognition of how important the implementation processes are seems to vary with the perceived immediacy of consequences. Although an individual manager may lose his job, a district health authority is unlikely to go out of business, however unsuccessful. Moreover, it can take many years for the effects of a policy to become visible and it is not always clear where the responsibility lies for relative success and failure. In these circumstances, ensuring a good balance is struck using all the components of the management of change is easier to see as desirable rather than imperative. Historically the NHS has invested heavily in strategy and structure and somewhat on systems; there have been weaknesses in the management investment in beliefs, management style and staff development. If the relationship between managerial cause and effect is clearer and the consequences of failure more visible, then the force of working on all these elements is compelling.

6 Strategic management is about the basic choice of what is crucial and deferring or refusing the rest – yet another balance to

be struck. This carries the twin temptations of biting off more than one can chew, or missing opportunities/ducking challenges. Perhaps it is a balance which cannot be got right – with hindsight it is easy to see that an important opportunity was missed or too much attempted in too short a time, or even both at once.

An established organisation with plenty of flexibility and room for manoeuvre built into its strategy has a better chance of coping with the unmissable opportunity or the unpredicted threat; and its environmental scanning should give it more time to accelerate or decelerate the key items on the change agenda as circumstances change.

7 Appropriately enough, a final thought about the development of strategic managers arising from the previous observations. Many of these are about various kinds of balances requiring a range of different kinds of sensitivity and personal insight. At the same time, management is a somewhat desensitising process because of the results orientation, exposure, pressure and inevitable conflicts.

Managers are constantly adopting postures – whether conscious or not – on all kinds of balances, such as tough/tender, fast/slow, do/consult, stick/carrot. Wishy-washy inertia clearly has to be avoided, but in the long run the Rambo posture is not going to deliver the best results either. It is not even possible to begin to make sensible choices about these balances without first becoming aware of their existence and nature. The desensitising experience of managing itself needs to be balanced with some sensitising about the results of choices made. Many of the successes of the effective strategic manager – making decisions about the unknowable, reading external and internal environments, ensuring capacity to change direction or pace – are simply not available to the Rambo school of management. Without throwing the systems and action babies out with the bathwater, we need to recognize the significance of sensitivity and intuition in effective management. The implications for staff development are profound.

8

Action research and development in strategic planning

DUNCAN K NICHOL

The first part of this paper presents a before and after case study of the involvement of consultants from the King's Fund College in the development of an alternative approach to strategic planning in a district health authority. The second part offers an analysis of the success of such an organisational development resource in producing fundamental change in the organisation.

Case study: Wirral District Health Authority

In 1982, two district health authorities in the Mersey Region, Liverpool and Wirral, were projecting very large overspending problems (in Wirral's case a possible £5,000,000 overspend or 10 per cent of its revenue budget). Although sharing this financial predicament, Liverpool presented as a health authority with very little coherent planning whereas Wirral was the most comprehensively planned district in the region. In 1978, the Wirral strategy had been drawn up with operational research help from the Department of Health and Social Security to assess the changes in service consequent upon the opening of a new district general hospital and the associated closure of up to 13 small units. The strategy was highly quantitative and based on centrally promulgated norms of service provision, with predetermined assumptions about increased utilisation of clinical resources leading to shorter lengths of stay and higher throughput. There was an apparent matching financial plan.

An unplanned and uncontrolled expenditure explosion followed the opening of the new district general hospital in 1982. At the same time, the district suffered a reduction in previous planning assumptions about financial growth over the decade. Instead of a real cumulative 1 per cent growth rate year on year for 10 years (approximately £5,000,000) the district could expect growth money from the region over the decade totalling £2,000,000, which would not be allocated in equal annual instalments and which was to be earmarked for developments in non-acute services. Further, the district was asked by the region to transfer £4,700,000 recurring revenue from its acute to its non-acute services.

This combination of internal control difficulties and externally imposed parameters presented a crisis in management of the district. Region suggested that an external organisational development (OD) resource, namely the King's Fund College, should be invited to make a contribution. Amongst other points the Region's interest was in testing, in an action research mode, the King's Fund's alternative approach to planning which was summarised at the time in the appendix at the end of this chapter (page 00).

The proposed OD consultancy was intended to assist the district in three main areas:

1 *Planning systems and processes* – to contribute towards a more flexible and discriminating model for managing planning options; revised planning processes involving clinicians, other staff and consumers; a revised long-term strategy which was performance-based.

2 *Accountability and control* – to establish broad statements of direction against which the district's progress could be monitored and the development of improved systems of management information.

3 *Organisation and individual management development* – to develop a programme for individual managers and proposals for organisational change designed to enhance the organisation's capacity to respond to change quickly and purposefully.

WHAT HAS HAPPENED SINCE THE OD CONTRIBUTION

The new approach that has been developed in strategic planning dictates that such planning occurs at the unit level (and at the sub-unit level in future) – that is, at the level of management where the service is provided. This should involve the regular negotiation of contracts with individual clinicians and other staff about the amount and quality of service to be provided within the resources available. Unit managers negotiate these contracts within total financial and manpower ceilings which they themselves negotiate with district managers and also within an overall strategic framework which seeks to maximise the unit manager's freedom of manoeuvre whilst ensuring movement towards the district's strategic objectives. This approach requires the organisation as a whole to have the capacity to manage its affairs without a conventional predetermined prescriptive plan.

MIXED SCANNING

The absence of such a plan does not mean that the organisation is floating freely or that there are no controls or sense of direction.

The conventional plan is replaced by a strategy and a host of little plans, contingency plans and other alternatives. Such an approach is necessary because of the nature of the environment in which NHS planning has to take place and in which NHS managers have to manage – a very turbulent and unpredictable environment as already rehearsed. For example, over the last two or three years managers have had to cope with pressures such as: efficiency savings/cost improvement programmes, manpower targets, failure to fund in full the effects of pay awards, performance indicator targets, contracting-out of hotel services to private contractors, revenue reductions, and advances in medical and other technology. None of these pressures could have been predicted and almost all have effected district short and long-term plans.

The approach undertaken in Wirral accepts the unpredictability of the future, and seeks to keep options open and to maintain flexibility. The approach is termed 'mixed scanning' and seeks to ensure that short-term decisions are robust against a range of possible futures.

To frame this process of bottom-up planning the health authority produced a document entitled *Parameters within which unit management groups are to plan the delivery of service for 1985/86*. In addition to covering revenue and capital allocations and manpower ceilings, the parameters set targets for recurring revenue savings and provided a pool of non-recurring revenue against which unit bids could be made. Performance criteria were specified for each unit in respect of activity levels and performance. A wide range of exciting proposals emerged from the units against this backcloth and the three unit management groups' plans have been consolidated into a district-wide plan for the health authority. A similar document setting unit parameters for 1986/87 has gone further in introducing financial incentives for units to take initiatives which advance the health authority's key strategic objectives.

Integral to this process, unit management groups are seeking to conclude clear and firm agreements with clinicians about activity boundaries – contracts between unit managers and individual consultants about the specific activity level which will be resourced.

Currently work is in hand to introduce a system of continual performance review at all levels in the organisation. As a first and interim step a methodology of variance analysis is being developed using selected services, illustrative of a wide range of potential problem areas of data collection, analysis and interpretation. For any comparison of actual and planned levels of performance to be valid and credible, the 'targets' and 'variances' must have certain basic characteristics.

Targets must be:

Feasible within a given set of constraints.

Agreed through discussion and negotiation with managers – not imposed – to cultivate a sense of 'ownership' of targets, thus engendering a commitment to their achievement.

Explicit in the sense that a movement away from the target should be unambiguous in what it tells about performance.

Variances must be:

Attributable to a specific individual who by his actions can control the activity.

Subject to corrective action through a management protocol which specifies the range/scale of management interventions open to departmental managers, for example, overtime control, staffing/grade mix, purchasing policies.

Differentiated between changes in the volume of activity (usually outside the departmental managers control but an issue which general managers must address) and changes in productivity/ efficiency of a management cost centre.

Of considerable help during the consultancy was the introduction of general management, centrally promulgated for the NHS against the background of previous dissatisfaction with a consensus style of management. The concept of general management emphasises the important principles of personalising responsibilities for planning, implementation and control of health authorities' objectives, emphasising a task-orientated approach to management and with maximum devolution of authority to the lowest possible levels in the organisation. This initiative was timely reinforcement of the efforts in Wirral to create a unit-centred organisation. Units were created as elements of district organisation, in a manner which best fitted the strategic objectives of the health authority and which only secondarily were consistent with professionally-centred structures. The units – which may be structured on institutions or care groups, as examples – are now to be led by unit general managers subject to regular accountability reviews for the performance of each unit. The involvement of unit general managers on the district management board enables them to bring operational perspectives to policy-making and brings policy formulation within the ambit of operational managers.

SUMMARY

In essence, the traditional, stylised and input-orientated planning process based on detailed forecasting, analysis and very precise 'picture painting' of the future had failed as a mechanism of control. It had not built commitment on the part of key participants in the organisation (senior managers and clinicians) to contingent courses of action, because it had not involved people at unit and sub-unit level in debating options or sought to reconcile different values and aspirations. Planning had developed as a discrete activity with its product imposed on the organisation. Enormous management energy was devoted from the top to trying to make the plan stick. But worse, as key resource parameters underpinning the plan changed, both the creators and receivers of the plan disowned its validity, blaming the changing environment for their problems.

By contrast, the 'mixed scanning' approach attempts to cope with uncertainty, complexity, and changing values and seeks to use planning as a learning process. Plans are statements or preferred options at a given point in time and are related to a whole range of assumptions about the environment, services, the economy, and so on. As the environment changes and assumptions are affected, managers/planners have to cope efficiently and still deliver desirable change. The emphasis is very much on keeping options open and on flexibility and innovation throughout the organisation but, most importantly, at the operational level. The planning process operates at a unit level with unit managers engaging clinicians and others in debate about desirable/necessary change. Later with management budgeting for clinicians and much better information, the process should be occurring at sub-unit level. The organisational structure has had to be modified in line with this process and so too has the managerial culture. Parallel work on tracking variances and particularly developing 'early warning' indicators is proceeding.

Organisational development

CHARACTERISTICS OF THE PROCESS OF CHANGE AND ACTION

In pursuing the underlying objective of the action research project of closing the gap between strategic intent and operational implementation, the sponsors and principle actors in the project had to balance the very sensitive interrelationships of the *how* of creating change as well as the *what* and the *why* – the process as well as the content and the context.

To produce the necessary ingredients to cause a sufficiently critical mass to be worried about the mismatch between present cultures, structures and strategies and future requirements, the stimulus of crisis (serious economic difficulties and reduced future resource expectations) had to be matched by determined and sustained managerial action to challenge traditional ways of thinking and acting and to legitimise new ideas. Tactics which were introduced to shake up the status quo included the use of change workshops to talk through new working methods and to recognise the need for new managerial skills. Changes to administrative mechanisms, the creation of working groups and opportunistic exploitation of situations were used to build commitment round new solutions.

Inevitably, the initial pace was slow, proceeding flexibly and experimentally, moving from broad concepts to specific solutions and on the way, neutralising opposition whilst building political support around particular ideas and approaches. In particular, there was a conscious attempt to move the organisation towards integrated rather than compartmentalised structures and processes, deliberately disturbing the existing power groups, and opening up more of the organisation to information previously guarded by a few.

It is relevant in summarising key aspects of this analysis to use Johnston's[1] four stages in the natural process of change, as referenced by Andrew Pettigrew[2] in his book: the development of concern; the acknowledgement and understanding of the problem; planning and acting; and stablising change. A number of aspects of the Wirral consultancy are common to this framework.

In the first two stages, the consultancy successfully built on the 'perspective, information and contacts of the early adopters ... to prepare more of a critical mass of people to help influence key power figures'. Also 'problem-finding, educating and climate and tension-building for change are long processes with many iterations, blocks, deadends, and unpredictable areas of movement'[3]. New leaders were drawn out and tested during the debate and management development workshops were used to develop a unity of purpose in senior managers.

Stage three was dominated by 'the contracting-negotiation exercise' surrounding the approach to planning and the introduction of general management and was underpinned by consistency and good communications between the project steering group and operating managers. At this point, local managers had taken over the project from the consultants, who continued to play a supportive and reinforcing role.

In future, the fourth stablising stage will need to ensure that 'reward systems, information flows, and power and authority distributions support the newly emerging state ... a critical part of the stabilisation process has to do with the development and choice of successors who will want to maintain the new situation, and more idealistically perhaps who will maintain and then initiate the changes themselves when external pressure on the organisation makes further change appropriate'.[4] At regional level there is also concern to know how we can transfer the lessons and messages of the Wirral action and research to other districts.

The strategic management approach suggests that the linkages between substantive strategy, system development, planning, accountability and management development are not merely technical. They are themselves strategic and need to be designed as the basis of the systematic development of the organisation. This can be demonstrated by looking at how training and management development interventions were designed in response to issues confronting Wirral District Health Authority.

WHY HADN'T EVENTS IN WIRRAL TURNED OUT AS ITS PLAN HAD PREDICTED?

The reasons relate to Pettigrew's 'management of strategic change' model.

The inner context of change – for example, the attitude of clinician stakeholders – was underestimated and the process of change was given insufficient attention. There was a feeling that the outer context – for example, the forward resource projections – could be made to conform to a previously predicted and stable course. This was manifest in the energy devoted to negotiating with the region about the mechanics of the resource allocation formula rather than developing real contingency options with key local stakeholders.

Analysis of these issues pointed to a training/management development need for exposing district officers to managing what they don't control and in circumstances where the process of how they get there is unclear. There was also a need for increased awareness-training about the possible implications of the external environment.

KEY ACTORS WERE LOCKED INTO STEREOTYPED POSITIONS

This was demonstrated through a reflex conflict of roles between region and district, between doctor and manager and between compartmentalised service disciplines. There was a preference for segmenting problems within traditional boundaries.

These problems pointed to a training/management development diagnosis of needs for:

1 Leadership:

to establish the legitimacy and clarity of objectives;
to convert the energies of conflict to partnership;
to push with courage and persistence on the things which really matter.

2 Unlearning old roles and processes:

to stir up vested interest groupings and to create new coalitions;
to establish learning as an important value in itself;
to develop the capacity for lateral creative thinking and to feed back this organisational learning into the management processes of the organisation.

3 People management:

to liberate rather than control;
to unlock creativity and provide space;
to inspire more leaders (the job can't be done from the region or district headquarters alone);
to change round the cast by planned movement, succession planning and ad hoc manoeuvres;
to work down through the organisation with new concepts, values and processes.

THE ABSENCE OF A CONSCIOUS BALANCE AND MIX OF APPROPRIATE STRATEGIES FOR CHANGE

There was an urgent need to move away from the traditional reliance on structure and systems strategy and service content strategy towards strategies for developing management processes, human capability and working on attitudes.

This pointed to the need for deeper conceptual ability to recognise the opportunities for deploying alternative strategies and a keen sensitivity in securing the right balance of strategies.

Conclusion

The training/management development diagnostic pointers which came out of Wirral, taken collectively, have stimulated the Mersey Region to think about how the lessons of that experience conceptualised can be disseminated across the region. To assist in this task and in collaboration with the NHS Training Authority, the region is embarking with its districts on a programme of recruiting inhouse management development advisers at a very senior level in the organisation to act as change catalysts. These individual management development advisers will gain collective strength from each other and support from planned links with external resources provided by the faculties of management development centres already working with the NHS and possibly by selected industrial contacts from outside the NHS.

Appendix

KING'S FUND CONSULTANCY – ALTERNATIVE APPROACH TO PLANNING

1 The King's Fund College faculty have, for some time, been propounding an alternative view of planning to that which underpinned the NHS planning system of the late 1970s. Put simply, the existing system, even as modified in the direction advocated by the King's Fund in recent years, exhibits the following characteristics:

a. It is based on forecasting and analysis; that is, it seeks to forecast a picture of a distant future, both in terms of the pattern of services and the values and policies underlying that pattern, and to analyse the best way of achieving that future.

b. It has a centralising effect, in that planning is regarded as a discrete activity performed by specialists, in which local management action, insight and information is the raw material from which a central plan is produced.

c. Essentially such planning is a means of control – over the future, over local management decisions and over the choice of goals and purposes.

2 The criticism is that the attempt to give shape to the future in this way is inherently impossible – our capacity for prediction is weak and very significant aspects of the future are outside our control. Moreover, the traditional model does not specifically address itself to conflicts of values between those concerned with the Service. It is argued that the emphasis should be on the following:

a. Planning should be concerned with essential strategic issues and not with day-to-day management. Examples of NHS strategic issues include:

i) decisions which constrain options for the foreseeable future – major capital investment, for example;

ii) decisions which impact on, or can be taken only in conjunction with, other organisations (for example, joint planning with social services);

iii) decisions which represent long-term commitments to one goal or purpose over others – for example, the introduction of a protected regional mental illness/mental handicap programme budget.

In this sense decisions on, for example, precisely how many trauma and orthopaedic beds a district should have in 1994/5, are not 'strategic', because any decision now will be falsified by changes in resources available, new developments in treatments or changes in public expectation. Development of such a service could, however, be subject to strategic guidelines – such as the proportion of expenditure on acute services will not rise; developments have to be funded by efficiency gains within the acute sector; or minimum performance should improve to the 'best' levels currently attainable elsewhere.

b. Planning should be concerned not with reducing uncertainty about the future but with managing the uncertainty which is bound to exist. In practical terms, this means giving managers at all levels the sense that a 'plan' does not relieve them of the responsibility for responding to changes in the environment as they occur. This implies that plans should be 'bottom up' and concerned with keeping options open rather than closing them down.

c. Planning – both the process and the product – must be evaluated. On this view, planning is a constantly evolving, learning process.

3 What sort of product does one expect from Wirral over the next year?

a. Revenue targets, derived from the region's resource assumptions which will be issued to Wirral as to other districts;

b. Commitments to the proportion of expenditure on different care groups or between different types of service (for example, hospital vs community);

c. Commitments to outside bodies – such as other health authorrities ('Wirral undertakes to place X number of MH patients from Southport and Formby in suitable community settings by 198?);

d. Commitments on cost improvement targets;

e. The proportion of the estate in condition A/B will rise by 198? to X per cent.

These statements would, in effect, be a Wirral-specific, more detailed (albeit more short-term) refinement of the general policy, resource, manpower and estate guidelines issued to the region as a whole. At this stage, they would not, however, do more than influence immediate short-term decisions and inform the next step, the review of existing services.

4 Review of existing services

The consultancy intend to review all services from a zero base, rather than plan for incremental growth. In that Wirral will use activity, finance and manpower indicators developed jointly with the region, they may be using the information issued to other districts in the form of suggested service targets. In practical terms, the results of the review will be expressed for each aspect of the service in terms of a workload or level of service (which may be more or less than at present) provided at a cost in real terms, giving specified amounts of revenue for use elsewhere or requiring certain additional support.

5 Strategic framework for service development

From these two steps comes the third which will consist of a refinement in the light of experience of the original statements of direction, and a policy for each service over the next three to five years expressed in terms of the level of service to be provided and the financial, manpower and estate resources required.

6 Monitoring and Evaluation

In simple terms, this means devising an easily understood system for informing health authority members, management and the region of changes in performance and progress in the right strategic direction.

7 Essentially, what Wirral will produce will be not that different from what some of the better other districts may produce. One difference will lie in the effort to involve all those affected by strategic planning in the development of plans and in the thrust towards individual and organisational development.

References

1 Johnston A V. Revolution by involvement. Accountancy Age, 7, 36, 17 September 1975: p 11.
2 Pettigrew A M. The awakening giant: continuity and change in ICI. Oxford, Basil Blackwell, 1985: p 473. And see Pettigrew A M. Managing strategic change (chapter 9 of this book. p 117.)
3 See 2: p 474.
4 See 2: p 476.

Managing change

Introduction

Organisational culture and managerial leadership are two contributing but frequently countervailing forces in the management of change. They can pose the manager with a practical dilemma. On the one hand, the culture of an organistion may be the very thing that the manager believes needs to be changed if the organisation is to make a purposeful response to emerging threats and opportunities. On the other hand, some would argue that changes that the manager proposes may only be possible if they accord with the organisation's core values, which may not welcome change at all – at least not in the culture or the behavioural patterns that they underpin. As a consequence, there is often a struggle in organisations between evolution and stability – a tension between having to take on new forms in order to survive while regarding the organisation as successful now largely because of the form it takes on now.

The participants in the Managers as Strategists seminar agreed that a key managerial responsibility in the implementation of change is to strike a balance between new initiatives and organisational maintenance. This requires ongoing and simultaneous diagnosis and development of the organisation's capabilities. It requires a holistic view of the interplay between the content and process of change. It also requires what Andrew Pettigrew, in his introductory paper to this sub-theme, calls the 'crucial link between the leadership role and the managerial role in creating change.'

Pettigrew's paper draws from his own study of decision-making and change in ICI, a large manufacturing firm, to offer lessons for health services managers. The paper provides a broad review of the literature on strategic change processes and argues that organisational changes do not occur in the linear manner that was once thought. Instead, strategic changes tend to happen in relatively short bursts of activity followed by longer periods of incremental adaptation and stability, and the ICI study is used to illustrate that point. In doing so, the case study highlights the interaction of crisis, leadership, perception, choice, and action in the management of change.

Considered in this light, the development of strategic change takes on the character of a political-learning process, in which unlearning of current values and core beliefs may be crucial. The top leadership role is to creatively exploit tensions within the organisation, to generate movement, to manage conflicts and to make change stick. The lessons for health managers are many, but at the centre of them all is Pettigrew's notion that content, process and context can be seen as a triangle of forces in the management of change. Ignoring any one of them may mean the difference between strategic intent and operational implementation.

Leonard Schaeffer's account of managing change in a large US health maintenance organisation focuses on the leadership role of top management. It describes the kinds of organisational tensions that face managers and the wide span of activities that often have to be undertaken in order to deal with them. In this case, rapid growth in a highly competitive environment brought new staff with little sense of the organisation's shared ideology. That compounded the strains on internal communication and financial systems, resulting in a loss of management control. The important insights that were gained from changing the organisation's direction relate less to what went wrong in the past and more to what managers need to do to avoid similar problems in future – a good example of how reflecting on practice can improve management.

Involving people throughout the organisation in the change process is a crucial part of balancing new initiatives and organisational maintenance. Richard Norling's paper about the need for change at California Medical Center Los Angeles shows how managers use process – including environmental assessment, planning and management development – to build networks, to identify new directions, and to instill a change-oriented culture. Such changes are not achieved without problems, nor without challenge to old ways of managing. Norling suggests that education and communication are critical roles for the top manager if others in the organisation ultimately are to share responsibility for change and develop a willingness to learn.

Schaeffer's and Norling's case studies represent a recognition which emerged during the seminar discussions that the leadership role in the change process cannot be underestimated. Top managers have to provide clear messages about the rationale and objectives of change. They have to enable and support the operational work of subordinate managers. And they have to maintain an overview of where the organisation is going and of how it is getting there. This is not a role for the recluse manager, nor for those from what Bob Dearden called the Rambo school of management. It requires openness and sensitivity, and a willingness to accept error as something from which one learns.

9
Managing strategic change
ANDREW M PETTIGREW

Introduction

For much of British business and commerce the past five years
has been an era of radical change. Unremitting pressure from
changes in their political, economic, and business environment
have caused many organisations to rethink their core purpose,
structure, and strategy and the content and style of implementation of their employment policies and practices. The sense of
business crisis around this latest recession has provided 'a window
for change', when 'the impossible' changes of the recent past
could be quickly carried through. The most visible and tangible
manifestations of this belated activity has been the desire of firms
to divest themselves of financially non-robust product lines, and
structural change in order to reduce numbers of employees and
get fixed costs down. Thus between 1977 and 1981 British Steel
cut its numbers employed by 47 per cent, Talbot Cars by 56 per
cent, BL Cars by 40 per cent, Courtaulds by 31 per cent, and
GKN by 30 per cent. Even Imperial Chemical Industries (ICI),
traditionally regarded as the blue riband of British manufacturing
industry, has reduced its numbers employed in the UK by 31 per
cent between 1979 and 1983, but over the same period has only
made a 3 per cent reduction in its employees working outside the
UK. The result is that in 1986 there are more people working for
ICI outside than inside the UK.

If the past several years has demonstrably been an era of change
the optimist would also argue it has also been an era of organisational learning – though it seems organisations like individuals
often acquire their most fundamental learning from exposure to
extreme situations. But what have been some of these areas of
learning? Undoubtedly one aspect of management learning has
been to do with the what, why, and how of creating strategic and
operational changes in large organisations. Strategic is being used
here just as a description of magnitude of alteration in, for example, market focus and structure, recognising the second order
effects, or multiple consequences of any such changes. Operational is taken to mean the necessary requirement to translate
broad strategic changes into alterations in manning levels, working practices, technology, and operator control at factory or unit
levels.

As we shall see in the case illustration of ICI which follows in this paper, one crucial aspect of creating strategic change is to do with *unlearning*, how large organisations can be encouraged to first challenge and then change their core patterns of belief and behaviour. Indeed it is a central argument of this paper that for major reorientations to occur in the firm's business strategy and structure, then major adjustments in the firm's *ideology* or *core beliefs* must happen. It is precisely because strategic changes involve the questioning and eventual displacement of an organisations central beliefs about itself in relation to its competitive environment, that such changes invariably require the force of sustained environmental pressure and the orchestration and vision provided by new business leadership.

So managing strategic change is not just a question of waiting for and then mobilising a receptive context. It also involves the role of executive leadership and managerial action in intervening in the existing concepts of corporate strategy in the firm, and using and changing the structures, cultures, reward systems, and political processes in the firm, both to draw attention to performance gaps resulting from environmental change and to lead the organisation to sense and create a different pattern of alignment between its internal characteristics, strategy and structure and its emerging concept of its competitive environment. The real problem of strategic change therefore is anchoring new perceptions of the environment, new issues for attention, new ideas for debate and resolution, and mobilising concern, energy, and enthusiasm often in an additive and evolutionary fashion to ensure these early illegitimate thoughts gain powerful support and are eventually implemented in a contextually appropriate manner.

Large firms have improved their capability to capitalise on environmental disturbances and to use executive leadership to facilitate the unlearning and reorientation of beliefs and behaviour. This is leading to professed desires to avoid strategic drift, the tendency to carry on using yesterday's strategic recipes for todays competitive environment.

Another feature of the recent learning behaviour of firms is a new interest in trying to connect business strategy and structure change with policy making and practices in the human resource management area. The present period of radical change has exposed real gaps in the managerial capability of firms to operate in new markets and technologies, and indeed to confidently and effectively manage change. One outcome of this process of learning has been the placement of management development as a central strategic issue for the firm.

One fundamental question all too frequently asked and rarely answered by the survivors of change in large firms is will we get caught out again? Do we have to wait for another business crisis and the next generation of John Harvey-Jones, John Egans or Lee Iacoccas before we'll wake out of our next slumber? More positively, how can we create the conditions in our firm so that change is a continuous process and not a series of revolutions interspersed with incremental adjustments? How can we unlearn and learn outside the enabling and energising circumstances of an extreme situation?

This paper has three main sections. Immediately after this introduction there follows a review of the theoretical and empirical literature on strategic change processes. The second section uses my own recent study of top decision-making and change in Imperial Chemical Industries (ICI)[1] to illustrate certain of the established patterns of knowledge about strategic change processes and to reveal some additional patterns and ideas suggested by the ICI data. The following section then moves on to consider some leadership and managerial tasks associated with the formulation and implementation of strategic change. This section also draws on the ICI study for illustrative example. The final section offers a summary of the paper and some very brief observations about managing change in the NHS.

The character of strategic change processes

Although it is always possible to find contrary examples both in different societies and in varying fields of enquiry, by and large social scientists have not studied the elite and powerful groups in the societies where they practice their skills. Why this happens is an interesting question but one too broad to ask and try to answer here. Looking for a moment at some of the most often quoted empirical studies of organisation power relationships it is clear that such studies are often confined to lower operatives and managers[2], or to specialist or advisory groups in business[3], or they are conducted in less central institutions such as universities.[4] A consequence of this is that some of the key processes of decision-making and change which involve those with high levels of positional power are shielded and lie unrevealed. A consequence of this shielding is that myths abound and are perpetuated about rational problem solving processes of formulating and then in a linear fashion implementing strategic change conducted by all-seeing and presumably omnipotent chief executives or general managers.

Thus in micro-economics strategic planning in organisations is conceived of as being dominated by powerful entrepreneurs. Meanwhile in some of the earlier views of business policy and planning [5,6] and even in later reformulations of that view[7], strategy formulation is still portrayed as a rational-linear process. As applied to the formulation of strategy the rational approach describes and prescribes techniques for identifying current strategy, analysing environments, resources and gaps, revealing and assessing strategic alternatives, and choosing and implementing carefully analysed and well thought through outcomes. Depending on the author, explicitly or implicitly, the firm speaks with a unitary voice, can be composed of omnipotent, even heroic general managers or chief executives, looking at known and consistent preferences and assessing them with voluminous and presumably apposite information, which can be organised into clear input-output relationships. Bourgeois and Brodwin have recently and appropriately labelled this the 'commander model' of formulating and implementing strategy.[8]

But does this 'commander' view of rational choice and change processes equate with what we know of top management behaviour? Does organisational action derive so singularly from decisions taken at the top, or do many senior executives find either the levers they are pulling being pushed and pulled in different directions by their peers or subordinates, or in the task of strategy implementation find the levers they are pulling not connected up to anything or anybody? Indeed is it the case that as far as senior executive behaviour is concerned, thinking big is not the same as acting big?

In the sphere of politics and government, March and Olsen's recent excellent review of the literature notes the phenomenon of a succession of US Presidents from Wilson to Carter generating and abandoning reorganisation plans.[9] Apparently there is a tendency for Presidents to experience cycles of enthusiasm and disappointment, for problems to be identified but not solved and for promises to be made but not kept, with all this reaping a harvest of frustration and disillusionment. March and Olsen derive two important conclusions from their review pertinent to the theme of this paper. Firstly they argue that long run developments of political institutions are less a product of intentions, plans and consistent decisions than they are a product of incremental adaptation to changing problems with available solutions within gradually evolving systems of meaning. Their second point is a corollary of the first: attempts at comprehensive reorganisation invariably fail; change often materialises as a product of continuous, incremental processes. In effect *changes* often fail while *changing* often succeeds because changing is not noticed whilst changes most certainly are.

While not taking on board the 'garbage-can' view of process implicit in March and Olsen's view of presidential or executive behaviour, Kotter's book on general managers[10] and Quinn's book on strategic change[11] both recognise the incremental and often intuitive character of executive behaviour and by implication some of the limitations of executive power. The agendas that Kotter's general managers generated were often vague, unwritten, only partially connected to implicit and explicit business strategies and were dependent on the availability of wide networks of relationship for implementation. Meanwhile Quinn conceives of strategic change as a cautious, step by step evolutionary process, a jointly analytical and political process in which executives muddle through with a purpose.[12,13]

Kanter's interpretation of innovation in the firm is that it is inhibited by the anti-change structures and cultures to be found in 'segmentalist' companies and facilitated by the change receptive contexts to be found in 'integrative' companies.[14] She also argues that change process management requires power skills, skills in persuading others to invest information, support and resources around new initiatives. Kanter's view of the politics of innovation is more explicitly laid out than Quinn's, arguing as she does that would be innovators have to compete in a market place for information and ideas, an economic market place for resources, and a political market place for legitimacy and support; but her overall characterisation of the process of change is very similar to Quinn's treatment of the subject where building awareness and credibility for new ideas, offering partial solutions, broadening political support,and overcoming opposition are all central activities.

The empirical process research published in the 1970s by, for example, Bower[15] and Mintzberg [16] and more recently by Quinn[17] and Kanter[18] has made a number of descriptive contributions to the understanding of strategic change processes. Strategic processes of change are now more widely accepted as multi-level activities and not just the province of a few, or even a single general manager. Outcomes of decisions are no longer assumed to be a product of rational or boundedly rational debates, but are also shaped by the interest and commitments of individuals and groups, forces of bureaucratic momentum, and the manipulation of the structural context around decisions and changes. With the view that strategy development is a continuous process, strategies are now thought of as reconstructions after the fact, rather than just rationally intended plans. The linear view of process explicit in strategy formulation to strategy implementation has been questioned and with that questioning has come both an additional awareness of the substantial but limited power of chief executives in implementing strategic change and new attempts to develop models and processes of implementation other than the simple commander model.[19]

STRATEGIC CHANGE AS A PATTERN OF REVOLUTION AND INCREMENTAL ADJUSTMENT

While Quinn's work captures well the additive, evolving, incremental character of strategic changes and in so doing clearly expresses the point that in the management of strategic change there are process limits to consider as well as just cognitive limits, the logical incrementalist approach of Quinn over-emphasises the continuous incremental nature of change and thereby conceals the major role that environmental disturbance and crisis can play as an enabler and trigger for significant change. Mintzberg[20], Miller and Friesen[21], and Miller[22], using a mixture of metaphors, all see strategic change occurring in spurts, revolutionary periods, or quantum leaps, each followed by a period of continuity. Although the work conducted at McGill University by Mintzberg and his colleagues usefully identifies both the ebb and flow of individual strategic concentrations in the firm and also the existence of periods of revolutionary and evolutionary change[23], what these authors do less precisely is to develop a process theory which links together the periods of high levels of change activity and low levels of change activity and thus begins to explain the timing, content, and relative intensity of those periods. Another approach, that again relies at least partially on a crisis theory of change which does have more to say about precrisis, crisis, and stabilisation, and thus about the linkages between revolutionary and evolutionary periods, is offered by Jonsson and Lundin[24], Starbuck, Greve and Hedberg[25], and Brunsson.[26] By introducing more explicitly into their analysis the importance of organisational ideologies and standard operating procedures both as inhibitors and – in the case of changing ideologies – as precipitors of change, these authors offer a more satisfactory way of explaining revolutions and evolutions, and the links between high levels of change activity and lower levels of change activity. Brunsson, in an elegantly written paper, argues that organisations periodically jump from one predominant ideology to another, and that radical changes have to be preceded by and initiated by ideological shifts.

To the question of how ideologies are changed, Brunsson answers as a result of a combination of externally driven crises, shifts in leadership, and the properties of ideologies themselves. The most stable ideologies are those which are vague and widely applicable; sharper, more definite and particular ideologies are easier to question and eventually debunk in the face of a changing reality. Crucially Brunsson also argues that the periods when ideological shifts are in process – when the dominant ideology has not yet been debunked and when any aspiring new ideology still lacks a critical mass of support – are poor contexts for action. This is because ideological inconsistencies increase uncertainty and make it difficult to marshall the strong commitments and high levels of motivation and energy which are necessary to create radical organisational changes. Thus Brunsson argues an ideological shift has to be completed before radical action in the change sphere can begin.

In what follows I shall use an illustrative example from a major study of ICI to provide confirmatory data both of the waxing and waning of particular strategies in the firm, and for the tendency of strategic changes to occur in radical packages interspersed with longish periods of absorbing the impact of revolutionary action and then of coming to terms with the fact that further changes are eventually necessary. Explicit in the presentation of the ICI data is the point that crucial to the timing of such radical actions are real and constructed crises, changes in leadership and power, and the transformation of organisational ideologies.[27, 28, 29]

The ICI study of strategic change

ICI is one of Britain's largest manufacturing firms and in 1981 ranked the fifth largest of the world's chemical companies in terms of sales in US dollars after Du Pont and the big German three of Hoechst, Bayer and BASF. The research examines ICI's attempts to change their strategy, structure, technology, organisational culture, and the quality of union management relationships over the period 1960–1984. An important and unusual feature of the research strategy has been the collection of comparative and longitudinal data. Interview, documentary, and observational data are available from ICI's four largest divisions and the head office of the company. These data have been assembled on a continuous real time basis since 1975, through retrospective analysis of the period 1960–1974, and in the case of the divisional chapters by probing into the traditions and culture of each division established long before the last two decades.

The study explores two linked continuous processes. The initial focus of the research was to examine the birth, evolution, demise and development of the groups of internal and external organisation development consultants employed by ICI in order to help initiate and implement organisation change. This analysis of the contributions and limitations of specialist led attempts to create change, has led to the examination of broader processes of continuity and change in ICI as seen through the eyes and activities of the main board of the company, and the boards of ICI's four largest divisions – Agricultural, Mond, Petrochemicals, and Plastics. The ICI study contributes to knowledge about the part played by very senior executives in corporate wide strategic changes, the role of divisional boards and directors in making division wide changes in structure, organisational culture and manpower, and the influence of specialist change resources of the internal and external variety in making changes happen. Throughout the study the emphasis is on describing and analysing processes of change in context. Illustrating why and how the content of particular changes and the strategies for introducing them are constrained by and enabled by feature of the traditions, culture, structure, and business of ICI as a whole and each of its divisions, and by gross changes in the business, economic, and political environment ICI has faced through time.

In this research on ICI it should be emphasised that strategic choice and change processes are not being studied by treating the unit of analysis as the single strategic decision or single attempt at strategic change. Strategic change processes are regarded as contextually related continuous processes with no clear beginning or end. Context is being treated here in two senses. Firstly, outer context refers to the economic, political, and business environment of the firm and the way changes in those factors help shape the market and competitive position of the firm relative to others operating in similar markets or industries. And secondly, inner context refers to the ongoing business strategy, structure, culture, and political context in the firm which help shape the management processes through which ideas for strategic change and transformation proceed. The analysis begins and ends with a refinement of the notion that formulating the content of any new strategy inevitably entails managing its context and process. Thus theoretically sound and practically useful research on strategic change involves the continuous interplay between ideas about the *context* of change, the *process* of change and the *content* of change together with skill in regulating the relations between the three.

The ICI study thus asks questions such as: What kind of

managerial processes inside the firm encouraged continuity and change? How and why and when was the need for change sensed, the acknowledgement and understanding of emergent competitive problems taken on board by early champions for change, and eventually by elements of the old and new power system of the firm? How also was planning and action in the sphere of strategic change finally justified, and what combination of environmental triggering and executive leadership eventually led to the implementation and stabilisation of change?

Five cases of strategic change are compared and contrasted in the study. Here it is only feasible to provide illustrative indications of the patterns in the process of one of those five cases – the one relating to the strategic development of the whole ICI group. In this case, as in all others, there is a clear pattern for the timing and intensity of strategic change to be associated with significant changes in the outer context of ICI. The limitations of the power of those who champion strategic changes appear to require the massive enabling opportunity provided by gross alterations in outer context.

An examination of the corporate development of ICI over the period from the late 1950s until 1984 reveals three periods of high levels of change activity. Two of these three periods, the ones between 1960 and 1964 and between 1980 and 1984 could be sensibly labelled as revolutionary periods in that they featured ideological, structural, and business strategy change, whilst the third period between 1970 and 1972 was a period of substantial if lesser change when further structural change was made and elements of the ideological and business strategy changes made ten years earlier were accelerated or de-emphasised. The periods in between these packages of changes were occasions for implementing and stabilising changes, and, most notably between 1973 and 1980, an era of organisational learning when ideological justification was prepared for the revolutionary break between 1980 and 1984. Each of these periods of high levels of change activity were associated with world economic recessions, with their associated effects on world chemical production, markets, and prices, and in turn on ICI's relative level of business performance.

Since 1958 there have been five years of peak profits followed by downturns of varying severity with each cycle lasting from four to five years. The improvement from trough to peak has been 82 per cent (1958–1960), 74 per cent (1961–1964), 92 per cent (1966–1969), 255 per cent (1971–1974), and 95 per cent from 1975–1979. The period from 1980 to 1983 evidenced a stepwise change in macro-economic trends, a sustained recession in the

UK, a dramatic downturn is ICI's profitability, and major structural, manpower, ideological, and business strategy change.

The two periods of revolutionary change between 1960 and 1964 and 1980 and 1984 were preceded by and further reaffirmed ideological shifts. On the first occasion, they were associated with the 1958 and 1961 economic and business downturns and on the second occasion the 1980–83 recession. They were also occasions when new business leadership was supplied by men who had not spent their whole career in ICI. In 1960 Paul Chambers (later Sir Paul Chambers), a former senior civil servant and the first non-technical man for some years, was appointed Chairman. He began to emphasise financial and commercial management skills in a management culture heavily preoccupied with science and technology. And in November 1981 the announcement was made that an ex-naval intelligence officer, John Harvey-Jones (now Sir John Harvey-Jones), was to be Chairman of ICI. His ideological contribution is emerging as a lessening of bureaucracy and centralisation in ICI, sharper business accountabilities, and a greater emphasis on entrepreneurial skills and continuous change into the 1980s.

Both revolutionary change periods witnessed organisational, structural and business strategy changes, with the structural changes occurring in a cumulative way over a relatively short time, and the business strategy changes emerging and being implemented rather more slowly *after* the ideological and structural changes had been justified and then introduced. One of the contributions of the ICI research is therefore to question Chandler's dictum that structure follows strategy[30], by indicating why and how business strategy change follows ideological and structural change.

Leadership tasks in creating strategic change

The highly synoptic and partial account of some patterns in ICI's corporate development described above has revealed an association between environmental change and pressure and internal strategic change. As such the view so far of strategic change is that real change requires crisis conditions and by implication senior executives who may be pushing for change in precrisis circumstances do not have sufficient leverage to break through the pattern of inertia in their organisation. However, although the above brief analysis does reveal periodic eras of high levels of change activity precipitated by crisis, it is not being argued that the process and content of strategic changes can be explained solely by economic and business related environmental disturbance. Clearly a potential danger of an analysis which might infer too simple a relation between economic and business crisis and organisational change is that the firm may thus end up being seen just 'bobbing on the economic waves, as so many corks on the economic bathtub'.[31] As I have already noted, no such brand of simple economic determinism is intended here. Behind the periodic strategic reorientations in ICI are not just economic and business events, but also processes of managerial perception, choice, and action influenced by and influencing perceptions of the operating environment of the firm and its structure, culture and systems of power and control. The antecedent factors and processes of the precrisis period are crucial to the character and content of the package of structural and then business strategy changes made at the revolutionary points when those changes are actually delivered. Crucial in the precrisis period is the process through which the dominating ideology nurtured in earlier contexts is first challenged and then changed. Since business strategies are likely to be rooted both in the idea systems which are institutionalised in an industry sector at any point of time[32, 33], and are represented in the values, structures and systems of powerful groups who control the firms in any sector, changing business strategies has to involve a process of ideological and political change which eventually releases a new concept of strategy which is ideologically acceptable within a newly appreciated context. It is precisely because this precrisis era of ideological change represents such a fundamental challenge to the dominating ideas and power groups of the organisation that such eras of ideological challenge are so often thwarted, sidetracked or otherwise immobilised, leaving many who have attempted to champion new ideas faced with stereotyping as odd balls, moral entrepreneurs or folk devils. Posed in this way the development of strategic change in the firm takes on the character of a *political-learning process*, a long-term conditioning and influence process designed to establish the dominating legitimacy of a different pattern of relation between strategic content, context, and process.

But how is this done, indeed prescriptively how can it be done? An approach to the practice of change management complementary to the findings of the ICI study is that propounded by Johnston.[34] Johnston's argument is predicated on three assumptions. The first of these is that some evolution is occurring in a natural way in most organisations. Second, that this natural evolution is in response to external pressures and is therefore retrospective and remedial, rather than preventive. And third, that any such change process absorbs a great deal of energy in the firm because it may require power redistribution, role changes, the abandonment of past practices and old ideologies, and restructuring. Building on these assumptions, Johnston makes an assertion highly compatible with the findings of the ICI study that development or change processes are often dependent on a few people, reactive to the general world, and can peter out or be reversed. A way to try to prevent such regression or reversals is to conceptually understand the evolution of natural processes of change in organisations and to help establish an organisation process of change with the necessary internal skills, actions, and systems to maintain development in the direction sought. Prescriptively this means in the broadest sense that the first step in the change process should be to improve and build on any natural processes of change by tackling questions such as how can existing processes be speeded up, how can conditions that determine people's interpretations of situations be altered, and how can contexts be mobilised to achieve practical effects along the way to move the organisation, perhaps additively, in a different strategic direction? Thus any adequate approach to managing change must be based on the principle of understanding the context, of knowing what you are dealing with, and of choosing as a starting point some area of movement that can be built upon.

THE PROCESS OF CHANGE

For all its oversimplifications, including the tendency to assume both discrete and exclusive categories and linear sequential development, Johnston's four stages in the natural process of change do usefully capture broad elements of the descriptive findings of change elaborated in the ICI research, and allow one to make sensible prescriptive statements about necessary leadership and management tasks at each of the four stages. The four stages are:

>the development of concern;
>the acknowledgement and understanding of the problem;
>planning and acting;
>stabilising change.

In fact the data from this study, particularly about the contribution of visionary leaders and early adopters in change processes, indicates the importance of an initial *problem-sensing stage* which may predate a stage of development of concern. In the sphere of strategic change, signalling problems as worthy of attention and getting those problems a legitimate feature of corporate discussion and decision-making is itself a time-consuming and politically very sensitive process. One of the contributions made by Lord Beeching and George Bridge in ICI in the 1960s, and by Harvey-Jones and Woodburn throughout the 1970s, was to sense and flag key problems worthy of management attention. From a political process point of view, it is critical not to rush prematurely from problem-sensing to planning and action in the change sphere. Actions recommended about problems which themselves are not yet accepted as legitimate topics of debate invariably produce the rejection of the change idea. The essence of the political learning process implied in this view of change is that individual sensing of problems must be complemented with activities which encourage some level of shared problem-sensing, spreading of development of concern about the emerging problem, and eventually broadly-based understanding of the problem, if novel ideas for change, are not to be imperilled at birth.

The development of concern stage assumes the presence of a small group of early adopters, or even – as illustrated in the ICI study – the presence of a single visionary change leader, sensing and imprecisely articulating a performance gap between the organisation's present condition and some feature or features of its operating environment. The key leadership task here is to more broadly educate the organisation by building on the perspective, information, and contacts of the early adopters. In effect, the task is to recognise the group doing this early sensing, to broaden the group by helping to connect them to peers, bosses, and subordinates with similar views, and to prepare more of a critical mass of people to help influence key power figures. This educational process may also involve getting unusual meetings going which cross existing organisational and departmental boundaries, help spread information and views, and integrate such data around particular issues or problems. Key line managers or consultants may also be able to set up meetings where power figures receive and test data, or personally to counsel individuals to act on the emerging views of the problem in parts of the organisation where at that point in time it is legitimate to do so. As the ICI study demonstrates, it can be valuable at this stage in the change process for deviants, even heretics, to think the unthinkable, and to say the unsayable, and for key line managers to be persuaded to help break traditional patterns of thought by setting up unconventional meetings where the process of discussing the previously undiscussable can begin.

In the next stage – the process of trying to get acknowledgement

and understanding of problems and issues which are emerging –
the key leadership task is to help the early adopters and key
power figures maintain and develop any structured dialogue
about the problem, and to avoid a tendency either to escape from
the problem by for example projecting it onto others, or to rush
precipitously into action before the present situation has been
carefully diagnosed, the change objectives have been clarified and
agreed, and a process has been planned to move from the present
to the desired future developed. This stage not only is critical in
terms of perpetuating any ideological change now in process, but
also is important in rational–analytical terms by exposing alternative diagnoses of the problem, exploring causes and generating
alternative solutions with reflections on their implications and the
development of criteria for choosing a solution.

The ICI data on strategic change suggests that the processes of
problem-sensing, educating, and climate and tension-building for
change are long processes with many iterations, blocks, deadends, and unpredictable areas of movement. Persistence and
patience in championing change seems to be necessary to initiate
and perpetuate this process of conditioning and influence, and
deliberative attempts to alter the structural and cultural context of
decision-making and capitalise on environmental disturbances
seem necessary to break out from mere acknowledgment and
understanding of problems into a stage of executive planning and
action. Because radical changes require strong commitments and
high motivations, they also presuppose the existence of ideological reorientations, and therefore the unequivocal availability
of a new ideology which precisely and enthusiastically endorses
the changes. Ideological reorientations can occur through the
above processes of climate-building and education but major ideological change also requires other deliberate management action:
efforts should be made to influence patterns of socialisation by
changing career paths and reward systems, visibly using the
newly-promoted as role models to additively signal behaviour
required in the new culture; retiral situations should be used to
combine portfolios and responsibilities previously divided and to
release energy along sub-parts of the change problem previously
deadlocked by individual power figures and sectional interests.
Ideological reorientation may also be facilitated by breaking the
global problem into actionable bits which reinforce one another,
and by creating temporary or permanent task forces, coordination
committees and business teams which resolve conflicts and imbue
enthusiasms and commitment for action around pieces of the
change.

Johnston's otherwise helpful prescriptive view of change management tends to underemphasise both management action to change, and thereby restructure the context in which change processes develop, and the extent to which effective action in managing strategic change is dependent on mobilising environmental disturbances and crises in order to achieve practical effects.[35] Gross change in the environment of the firm can be orchestrated and capitalised upon to create opportunities for organisational learning, to destabilise power structures, and connect previously unrelated solutions around now more precisely stated and more enthusiastically supported organisational ideologies. But if crises provide ideological closure and therefore justification for action, it is evident that some organisations are more likely to be able to capitalise on the 'window for change' provided by environmental disturbances than others. Here, of course, what has or has not happened in the precrisis circumstances may crucially affect the quality of planning and action taken to implement strategic changes. Paradoxically the delays and incremental movements in the problem-sensing and development of concern and acknowledgment and understanding of problems stages may have not only sensitised a wider set of people to the incipient problems, and enabled debates to occur around a variety of solutions, but also helped to draw out and test new leaders possibly with the capabilities to manage the new circumstances or, if not, with the opportunity to use temporary structures and administrative mechanisms to prepare the ground for new patterns of organisation. The ICI data also demonstrates how management training and development experiences can be used in the pre-crises situation to develop a common language for thinking about change management, and to increase the capability and confidence of managers to carry through operational change management tasks delegated to them by senior executives.

THE TOP LEADERSHIP ROLE

The planning and acting tasks in change management have been well codified and described in the concepts and techniques reported in Beckhard and Harris[36] and Beer.[37] These demonstrate the importance of defining the present condition of the organisation in relation to its changing environment, of clarifying the desired future state for the organisation in relation to its changing environment, of building commitment around particular change objectives, and of appointing transition managers to move parts of the organisation from the present through the transition state to the change objective by means of detailed and contextually sensitive action plans. The ICI data also reveals how this operational process of change management is greatly facilitated by unity of philosophy and purpose amongst the senior executives leading the change process. Giving clear, simple messages and maintaining those consistently and without dilution within a broad philosophy justifies and conceptually holds together a series of change initiatives.

If the top leadership role at the action stage in change management is to put tension into the organisation by providing a clearly articulated rationale for change and some consistently stated change objectives, the operating management responsibility is to plan and organise the use of this tension to generate movement. Here, agreeing the targets of change and the form and timing of their publication is important. The publication process is really a contracting-negotiation exercise which takes into account the different positions of individual units, deals with possible differences in interpretation of the leadership message, and manages apparent conflicts in the implications of the messages. There is clearly a monitoring task to ensure progress, and a support task to ensure that problems inhibiting progress are dealt with creatively and ethically, and that operating managers are provided with a 'political umbrella' for the risks they have to take.

A key to success in these kinds of change activities is the effective management of the links between the senior group leading the change and the operating managers carrying through the details of implementing particular changes. Even in crisis-driven circumstances the operating management role is likely to involve detail and grinding on over time, and is very dependent upon the leadership role being consistently maintained. If someone in an operating management role is close to acceptance of hard targets in his sphere of negotiated influence, his work could be undermined and even destroyed by a weakening of the leadership position.

But the ICI study also indicates that strategic change is not just a question of justification and initial action, of making things happen, it is also a question of making things which happen stick. Making changes stick requires the additional management task of stabilising changes, of making sure that reward systems, information flows, and power and authority distributions support the newly emerging state. Since changes are often initiated by or otherwise associated with key figures, and changes often remain as long as those key figures remain, a critical part of the stabilisation process has to do with the development and choice of successors who will want to maintain the new situation and, more idealistically perhaps, who will maintain and then initiate changes themselves when external pressure on the organisation makes further change appropriate.

Summary and conclusion

The above case study and commentary has conceptualised strategic change in large organisations as a political learning process. Emphasis has been given to the role of environmental pressure and executive leadership in opening up and energising systems for change. Due attention has been given to the leadership role in change – broadly conceived of as problem-sensing, climate-building, vision-building, and tension creating, and the role of managers in contracting for, communicating about, and achieving change objectives. The crucial link between the leadership role and the managerial role in creating change was also highlighted. Finally the paper has also emphasised the role of internal and external consultants in helping key power figures champion novel ideas for change. This role can involve:

1 Helping power figures conceptualise strategic change processes.

2 Preventing early champions for change prematurely proclaiming solutions to strategic problems before the rest of the power system has sensed there is a problem which requires a solution.

3 Helping early adopters of change to build on the perspective, information and contacts they have to educate the organisation about the need for change.

4 Encouraging change by getting unusual meetings going which cross existing structures and boundaries and thus help integrate data, people and problems.

5 Encouraging deviants and heretics out into the open to say the unsayable and think the unthinkable.

6 Counselling power figures to expect deadends, iterations, blocks, and unpredictable areas of movement in long-term change processes and thus the requirement for persistence and patience in change management.

7 Encouraging minor changes in the internal structural and cultural context of the organisation which reinforce the direction of change being pushed.

8 Encouraging managers and planners to break broad strategic aims into manageable and therefore actionable bits.

9 Facilitating the creation of varied and appropriate communication mechanisms to ensure that a clear and consistent vision is communicated effectively down through the management system and between management and employees in operating units.

MANAGING CHANGE IN THE NHS: SOME BRIEF OBSERVATIONS

The preceeding descriptive and prescriptive points are largely based on my experience as a researcher, consultant, and trainer in business and commercial organisations in the UK and Continental Western Europe. Can knowledge and experience acquired from research and consultancy in business organisations be applied to the change management problems in the NHS? At the level of concept and principle the answer is probably yes. Indeed, Duncan Nichol's chapter[38] uses concepts developed in business settings to interpret experience of managing change in the Wirral District Health Authority. However, attempts to generalise about the *process* of managing change are always subject to conditional statements about the *content* and *context* of change. This is one of the difficult conundrums in trying to generalise about the practice of change management – contexts are so variable whether within the NHS, or between the NHS and business firms.

From my limited experience as a researcher and management consultant in the NHS it seems the jugular management problem of these times is closing the gap between strategic intent and operational implementation. In an era of management by performance, achieving outcomes is a critical management requirement. Closing the gap between intent and implementation is no longer 'a nice to have' but for the general managers an essential criterion of management performance and success.[39]

Why there is this problem of a gap between strategic intent and operational implementation is a fascinating question, but finding ways of closing it is a more worthwhile endeavour. Planning, of course, was to have been the cornerstone of the management of purposeful change in the NHS, but I sense as much self doubt and disillusionment with planning in the NHS now as there is at the very highest levels of big business.

The model of a triangle of forces in Figure 2 is relevant to why strategic intentions or plans are not implemented.
The three elements in the model briefly are:

1 Content – the areas or leverage points for change, frequently in business contexts identified through various analytical and quantitative techniques.

2 Process – the strategies, tactics, mechanisms and interactions about how change is managed.

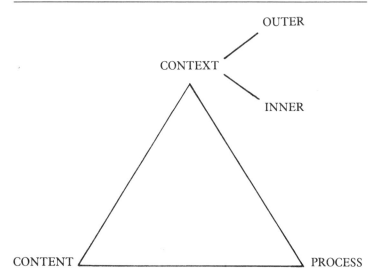

Figure 2   Broad analytical elements in managing change

3 Context – the environment within which change takes place. This can be further divided into: outer context, the factors outside the organisation such as changes in social, economic, political, and business environment; inner context, features of the internal environment of the organisation such as structure, culture, and small 'p' political context for change

A tension or triangle of forces can be identified between these three elements. Planning, particularly in business, typically has been concerned with the left hand side of the triangle. Enormous fact-gathering and analytical attention has gone into exposing alternative content areas for change in relation to established or establishing trends in outer context. However, insufficient attention to process and inner context reaps its harvest in problems of acceptance within the organisation.

The recognition that the management of any particular strategic change requires close attention to the interrelationship between context, content and the process for managing change, and that this recognition might provide clues to dealing with the problem of acceptance is the thread that many a business planner holds onto for the future.

But if my pessimism about closing the gap between strategic intent and operational implementation in the NHS rests on its devotion to the activity of planning, my optimism derives from the wider set of managerial activity implied in Figure 3.

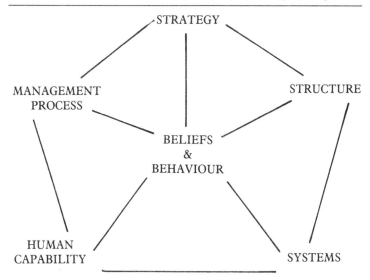

Figure 3   Management levers for change

Figure 3 represents a summary model of the management levers which can be pulled to exert pressure and support for change.

In the past, attempts to effect change in the NHS have failed because of an over-reliance on pulling the structure lever, when the fundamental change problem was and is changing beliefs and behaviour. At present there is a greater possibility of fundamental change, not only because of clarity, consistency, and persistency of environmental pressure, but also because the strategy, structure, systems and human capability levers are being pulled simultaneously and in a manner complementary and reinforcing of one another. Evidence from other kinds of large organisations suggests that it is only through such sustained pressure subtly exerted through a variety of complementary strategies that any real impact can be made on changing beliefs and behaviour.

(Since this paper was written, the National Health Service Training Authority and nine of 14 Regional Health Authorities in England and Wales have agreed to fund a research project on the management of change at district level. The work will be carried out at the Centre for Corporate Strategy and Change, University of Warwick, under Andrew Pettigrew's direction. The results of the research will begin to emerge during 1987 and 1988.)

References

1 Pettigrew A M. The awakening giant: continuity and change in ICI. Oxford, Basil Blackwell, 1985.

2 Crozier M. The bureaucratic phenomenon. Chicago, Chicago University Press, 1964.

3 Pettigrew A M. The politics of organizational decision making. London, Tavistock, 1973.

4 Pfeffer J. Power in organizations. Marshfield, MA, Pitman, 1981.

5 Ansoff H I. Corporate strategy. New York, McGraw Hill, 1965.

6 Andrews K R. The concept of corporate strategy. Homewood, Illinois, Irwin, 1971.

7 King W R and Cleland D T. Strategic planning and policy. New York, Van Nostrand, 1978.

8 Bourgeois L J and Brodwin D R. Strategic implementation: five approaches to an elusive phenomenon. Strategic Management Journal, 5, 1984: pp 241–64.

9 March J G and Olsen J P. Organizing political life: what administrative reorganization tells us about organizations. Administrative Science Quarterly, 7, 1983: pp 349–64.

10 Kotter J P. The general managers. New York, The Free Press, 1982.

11 Quinn J B. Strategies for change: logical incrementalism. Homewood, Illinois, Irwin, 1980.

12 Ibid

13 Quinn J B. Managing strategies incrementally. Omega, International Journal of Management Science, 10, 6, 1982: pp 613–627.

14 Kanter R M. The change masters: innovation for productivity in the American corporation. New York, Simon and Schuster, 1983.

15 Bower J L. Managing the resource allocation process. Cambridge, MA, Harvard University Press, 1970.

16 Mintzberg H. Patterns in strategy formation. Management Science, 24, 9, 1978: pp 934–948.

17 See 11.

18 See 14.

19 See 8.

20 See 16.

21 Miller D and Friesen P. Structural change and performance: quantum vs piecemeal – incremental approaches. Academy of Management Journal, 25, 4, 1982: pp 867–892.

22 Miller D. Evolution and revolution: a quantum view of structural change in organizations. Journal of Management Studies, 19, 2, 1982: pp 131–151.

23 Greiner L E. Evolution and revolution as organizations grown. Harvard Business Review, 50, 4, 1972: pp 37–46.

24 Jonsson S A and Lundin R A. Myths and wishful thinking as management tools. In: Nystrom P C and Starbuck W H (eds). Prescriptive models of organisations. Amsterdam, North Holland, 1977.

25 Starbuck W H, Greve A and Hedberg B L T. Responding to crises. Journal of Business Administration, 9, 2, 1978: pp 111–137.

26 Brunsson N. The irrationality of action and action rationality: decisions, ideologies and organizational action. Journal of Management Studies, 19, 1, 1982: pp 29–44.

27 Pettigrew A M. Patterns of managerial response as organizations

move from rich to poor environments. Education Management Administration, 2, 1983: pp 104–114.

28 See 1.

29 Pettigrew A M. Examining change in the long-term context of culture and politics. In: Pennings J M (ed). Organizational strategy and change. San Francisco, Jossey-Bass, 1985.

30 Chandler A J. Strategy and structure: chapters in the history of the American industrial enterprise. Cambridge, MA, MIT Press, 1962.

31 Boswell J S. Business policies in the making. London, Allen and Unwin, 1983.

32 Grinyer P H and Spender J C. Recipes, crises and adaptations in mature businesses. International Studies of Management and Organizations, IX, 3, 1979: pp 113–33.

33 Huff A S. Industry influences on strategy reformulation. Strategic Management Journal, 3, 1982: pp 119–131.

34 Johnston A V. Revolution by involvement. Accountancy Age, 7, 36, 17 September, 1975: p 11.

35 Ibid

36 Beckhard R and Harris R. Organizational transitions: managing complex change. Reading, MA, Addison Wesley, 1977.

37 Beer M. Organization change and development: a systems view. Santa Monica, California, Goodyear, 1980.

38 See Nichol D. Action Research and Development in Strategic Planning, (chapter 8 of this book, pp 91–102).

39 Pettigrew A M. Summary of proceedings of workshop on the management of change and manpower development in the NHS. Warwick University, 17–19 May, 1985.

10

Managing change in health care

LEONARD D SCHAEFFER

The rapid changes taking place in the health care system in the United States are well known. Health care is subject increasingly to two pressures that have not been present in the past. Consumers are demystifying health care and demanding more sensitivity to their own service and health care needs as they perceive them. At the same time, payors – especially employers and government– are becoming more price conscious and demanding lower costs and greater efficiency.

The health system is responding with an evolutionary and sometimes revolutionary transformation from a cottage industry to more organized systems for financing and delivering care. Physicians, hospitals, health maintenance organizations, and insurers are all developing vertically and horizontally integrated systems to respond to and capitalize on the demand for more organized, sensitive and efficient care and service.

The Group Health example

The Twin Cities of Minneapolis and St Paul are at the forefront of the health care revolution in the United States, with more than 40 per cent of the population now enrolled in one of six competitive health maintenance organisations (HMO's). Group Health serves as a good case study of this revolution because it has already had to respond to what other health organizations will eventually confront when competition intensifies in their communities.

Group Health is the largest HMO in the US Midwest. It was founded in 1957, with its roots established some two decades earlier in the 1930's. It was based on an ideological commitment to comprehensive, prepaid care. It was organized in opposition to the then existing medical establishment, and was met with strenuous opposition from that establishment.

Group Health's founders and original staff were true pioneers. As a result, the organization benefited from a number of unifying and motivating factors. The founding staff had a shared value system, which was based on their ideology and their self image as innovators. They had exellent and easy communication throughout the organization as a result of operating in a single location. They felt a sense of urgency, and had great internal cohesion, fostered in part by the vehemence of the external opposition. And, finally, they had a unique product. These pioneers faced a difficult struggle for survival, but succeeded because they had one of the most critical ingredients for market success – they were first, and they were right.

In the 1960's and 1970's, the organization grew rapidly, and with that growth came complex problems. Management systems that had proven sufficient for a small organization were not adequate to manage a $100 million company, and financial control was lost. The growth in the size of the company – the number of staff and the number of locations – made internal communications much more difficult. As the daily interactions required to maintain a sense of shared direction and values diminished, new staff were added who had no sense of the organization's history or ideology. Finally, the success brought imitators and competition to the Twin Cities. It was no longer good enough to be the first and to be right.

CHALLENGE OF THE 1980S AND GROUP HEALTH INC'S RESPONSE

Three challenges faced Group Health in the early 1980's as a result of its growth, complexity and competition: first, to restore management control to assure our financial viability; second, to reinvigorate our corporate culture, and re-establish a sense of shared values and direction; and finally, to understand and respond to the rapidly changing environment.

Group Health began to address each of these issues in 1982. First, we restored management control, and did it quickly. Group Health had lost money in 1981 for the first time in 13 years, so it was possible to focus all staff on the pressing financial situation. The financial crisis was successfully invoked to motivate substantial change.

We devoted much analytic time to determining our true revenues and costs, and then assigned responsiblility for those revenues and costs to managers throughout the organization. We automated our accounting and budgeting systems, set budgetary targets, strictly monitored variances each month, and hit our year-end budgetary targets. We accomplished all of this in six months, through a directive, arbitrary, top-down management process.

We then addressed the need to reinvigorate the corporate culture through a longer term, more collegial process of defining our mission, setting long-term goals, and articulating the values which should motivate our individual and corporate behavior. That process took an additional year and involved the Board and a large number of staff to assure input and support for the final products.

We also established new communications systems to address the needs of a complex, multi-site organization (16 locations, 2000 employees). Written communications include a monthly *President's Report* to all staff which describes our performance in key areas and reviews important issues; a monthly publication called *Staff Notes* which discusses internal events, personnel, and clinic information; and periodic memos as issues arise. All serve to provide regular and consistent information.

The communication system also includes a structured meeting schedule which provides staff with regular opportunities to interact, and serves as a forum for communicating important corporate messages. The President meets regularly with all vice presidents, the senior staff, the medical management council, including medical department heads, a medical operations committee and the management staff. In addition, the President visits each clinic, each medical department, and specific functional groups at least once a year. The President's meeting schedule serves as a model for staff throughout the organization. Each division head and manager has a comparable schedule structured to provide ongoing forums for communications and decision making.

The third major challenge was to try to understand the rapidly changing environment and develop a plan for the future. We put in place the first long range planning process at Group Health, and developed the first three-year plan for the future in late 1983.

In short, our response to the challenge of the 1980's was a fairly classic management response, and we achieved much of what we set out to achieve. By examining the results, we can identify some lessons and issues for managing change.

Lessons

First, we learned that the environment is changing much more rapidly than we envisioned. We responded vigorously to the 1982 data and set our course given the competitive environment as we understood it in 1983. But the environment changed dramatically, and the competition did not stand still.

The lesson is simple. We have to continually anticipate the future. In health care in the United States, all things seem to be changing all the time. A written plan is not the answer – to remain viable, a health care organization requires an ongoing process of assessing the environment, predicting future trends, identifying options, monitoring the effectiveness of current activities, and revising plans. In a competitive environment, a health care organization must develop an ongoing capacity to continually respond to and manage change.

Second, we learned that in health care, as in other service industries, the customer is always right. This is a difficult concept for health care providers. Health care professionals typically see their job as diagnosing and treating medical needs, and they do that well. However the old process of unilaterally diagnosing a problem and prescribing treatment is not enough in an increasingly competitive environment. Patients expect service, courtesy, communication, and understanding – not just quality medical care. Our market research shows that patients take quality of care for granted. What they want in addition to quality is a caring and reassuring attitude on the part of all staff, involvement in treatment decision-making, and no service hassles. The lesson is that we must meet service expectations as well as medical needs.

Third, we learned that in times of rapid change, new management staff who enter an organization as change agents – vitally necessary for challenging and changing institutions – can cause debilitating bureaucratic abrasion with existing staff. This occurs not just with the old line staff, but often even more with the previous year's change agents. The lesson is one that studies of government help us to understand, because the problem of turnover in top management confronts government more than other organizations. We need a commitment by all staff to understand the history of people, institutions, and issues. It is a two way street – we must understand newcomers and their history and values, and assure that there is an orientation for new staff and a commitment from them that they will work to understand the people and the institution they are joining.

Fourth, we learned that large organizations can make change difficult in two ways. Corporate structures can buffer staff from market realities. Corporate staff can generate analytic information about competition and circulate it to staff on an ongoing basis, but analytic information is not enough. Staff must see and feel competition in their daily activities.

Large institutions also can frustrate change by their size, complexity, and bureaucratic inertia. A consultant recently defined organizations for us as entities designed to prevent change. The solution is to develop individual and smaller unit identifications, heighten sensitivity to market forces, and foster responsiveness and accountability.

Fifth, we continually learned that professional staff – especially

physicians – do not react well to traditional corporate management techniques. Researchers throughout the world are identifying the need for staff autonomy and participation in decision
making. This is especially important in health care because the
medical professionals are trained to see their roles as an autonomous decision-makers. The ego strength required to make a series
of daily treatment decisions, including very serious medical decisions in some cases, may cause difficulties in large organizations
where teamwork and consistent procedures are important ingredients for success.

The work of Andre L Delbecq and Sandra L Gill illustrates this
issue well.[1] Their studies find that physicians do not respond to or
respect a hierarchial, appointed structure. They point out that as
issues become difficult or threatening, physicians become less
collegial and more autonomous – the opposite of what managers
tend to do in large organizations. Their desire is for maximum
influence on decisions with minimum direction from others or
participation in problem solving. The lesson and challenge to all
of us is to identify means to involve staff in decision making
through what Delbecq and Gill describe as representational structure and visible decision processes.

The health system as a management laboratory

A final point to review briefly is that what we learn about managing change in health care may serve as a model for other
organizations in other industries. Health care in the United States
has usually been regarded as unmanaged and therefore not a
management model. However, the opportunity now exists for
health care managers to step to the forefront of managing change,
because the health industry exemplifies and magnifies many of the
challenges confronting organizations throughout society. These
common challenges are:

Increasing competition is occurring in many other industries as
well as in health care, and is characterized by heightened sensitivity to the demands of the consumer, coupled with increasing pressure on prices and costs.

Health care exemplifies the pluralistic mix of public and private
sector involvement and interaction that is becoming common
throughout society.

Health care is prototypical of a labor intensive service industry
which forces the understanding of the organization as a human
system.

Health care is dominated by professional staff – physicians – who exemplify the performance, independence and attitudes of staff who earn their living with their minds, not their muscles, in much the same ways as other professional, white collar workers. All industries confront this issue to some degree, and need to learn how to respond.

Health care, like other industries, is currently facing an explosive growth of new technology.

Health care forces us to confront difficult ethical decisions in allocating care and resources.

Finally, health care is undergoing industrial restructuring and consolidation like other American industries, in the context of staff and institutional over-capacity, and continuing under-service to about ten percent of the population.

The traditional image of the 'well managed' private corporation may not be as well managed as we once thought (typified, for example, by the big three automobile manufacturers' reaction to competition from Japan). Because of the revolutionary changes in health care, we are being forced to respond rapidly and to develop approaches to manage the change confronting us – more quickly than most other industries. As a result, we have the opportunity to make a quantum leap from the ranks of the 'unmanaged' to the cutting edge of the management of change.

Change will remain the one constant in health care. Managing that change will allow us to continue the mission we share: to provide high quality care at an affordable price.

Reference

1 Delbecq A L and Gill S L. Justice as a prelude to teamwork in medical centres. Health Cove Management Review, Winter 1985.

11

Networking for change management strategies
RICHARD A NORLING

The health industry in the United States is undergoing a profound transition from a quasi public utility to an intensely competitive private sector market. The combination of limited
deregulation with increasing competition is widely forecasted to
bankrupt 10–20 per cent of America's 6500 community hospitals
by 1990.[1]

In 1984, US hospital revenues grew by only 5.6 per cent, well
below the industry's double-digit growth rates for the past ten
years.[2] More sobering still, 11,000 hospital beds were closed in
1984, the first time US hospital bed supply had not increased
since the American Hospital Association began keeping records.
The average length of a hospital stay dropped by a full day in the
past two years, and hospital occupancy fell to 66 per cent nationwide, an all time low. It would be fair to state that the US hospital
industry is entering a recession.

The State of California is in the forefront of these changes
sweeping across the hospital industry. California is a 'bell-wether'
state, according to futures watchers like John Naisbitt.[3] Fewer
than 60 per cent of California's hospital beds are occupied, and
the slump is deepening. What happens here may soon affect the
rest of the nation.

In California, deregulation set the wave of competition in
motion when legislative barriers to selective provider contracting
were removed in 1982.[4] The State of California moved quickly to
set up a competitive bidding process for the $4 billion 'Medi-Cal'
health care program for the low-income population. The state's
Medi-Cal purchasing agent, nicknamed the 'Czar' for his broad
powers, selected only 238 of the state's 600 hospitals. The selection was made primarily on price per day of hospital care. The
state's action triggered new rounds of hospital price wars, as Blue
Cross and other major health insurance carriers negotiated new
contracts with selected hospitals. These 'preferred' hospitals won
their designations by agreeing to disounts of 15–30 per cent in
prices.

The California health care marketplace is unique in other important ways.[5] Enrolment in health maintenance organizations,
which contract for a comprehensive package of health services, is
more than 40 per cent of those under age 65 in the San Francisco

Bay area, and has penetrated more than 30 per cent of the enormous Los Angeles market. Investor-owned hospital chains are better established here than any other state. More than one hospital in three in Los Angeles is owned by a for-profit corporation. These for-profit hospitals have a reputation for higher cost services and 'skimming' upper income customers, avoiding treatment of their share of the community's low income residents.[7]

Deregulation of California's hospitals is widening. The state's 'Certificate of Need' law regulating the number and location of hospitals has been terminated, effective January, 1987. This is likely to trigger a new hospital building boom, as for-profit hospital chains expand into new markets.

At the same time, there are changes occurring in medical practice. It is difficult for those outside the health industry to appreciate the significant and unique role of the physician in health care organizations like California Medical Center Los Angeles.[8] In the US, most physicians are independent entrepreneurs. Physicians ally themselves with hospitals voluntarily and without compensation. In California, it is still against the law for a hospital to directly employ a physician for patient care purposes. Their 'privileges' to practice medicine within hospitals are exchanged for the patients they bring to the facility. Without a strong and active medical staff, no hospital can operate.

Physicians are experiencing a business downturn, just as are hospitals. Some specialties report a 15–25 per cent decline in patient volume and revenues. There is a surplus of physicians in America; an estimated 90,000 doctors will be unneeded by 1990.[9] An estimated 12 per cent of California's 57,000 physicians are considered surplus.[10] At the same time, major health care payors are attempting to restrict physician fees. The federal government has imposed a moratorium on increases in physician payment under Medicare, and the ceiling could be made permanent.

Two further underlying forces are driving hospitals and physicians towards the private sector marketplace model: first, the new attitude of wellness in the minds of consumers de-emphasizes the centrality of hospitals in the health care marketplace. Second, those who pay for health have shifted from retrospective cost-reimbursement to prospective payment only to 'preferred' providers who compete on price. Gaining preferred provider contracts is creating a new distinction between the 'haves' and 'have nots' among California hospitals, as patient choice is increasingly limited by the health insurance carriers.

California Medical Centre Los Angeles (CMCLA)

California Medical Center Los Angeles is a 325-bed acute-care hospital established nearly 100 years ago. It is the founding hospital of the Lutheran Hospital Society of Southern California (LHS), a multi-hospital system which owns or manages seven facilities. LHS is the oldest multi-hospital system in California, and founding member of a new alliance of non-profit hospitals, American Healthcare Systems, whose 31 corporate members own or are affiliated with 1,191 hospitals nationwide. LHS has a reputation for managerial innovation, providing California Medical Center Los Angeles with a unique perspective and opportunities for development.

In comparison with other Los Angeles hospitals, California Medical Center Los Angeles is large and busy. In 1984, 12,479 admissions generated 77,036 patient days and $56,838,000 in total revenues. The emergency room is the most active private facility in the city; only the county hospitals handle more paramedic ambulance emergency patients in Los Angeles.

The urban location of California Medical Center Los Angeles is both advantage and liability. The hospital is only eight blocks from the central business district, location of the corporate headquarters of a dozen of California's top 100 companies, including ARCO, Security Pacific National Bank and Transamerica Occidental Life Insurance. Urban renewal and private development are revitalizing the city center, with more than four billion dollars of new commercial and residential development under construction.

A major rebuilding program is in progress at CMCLA which will replace all but 75 of the hospital's beds in a 9-story state-of-the-art patient care tower. In a competitive marketplace, the new facilities will present a state-of-the-art image which matches the rebuilding boom now underway in the Los Angeles central business district.

Growth has yet to touch the blighted neighborhoods of South Central Los Angeles which also adjoin the hospital. The hospital currently serves some of the most neglected Spanish-speaking and black low-income populations in Los Angeles. In 1984, more than 25 per cent of the hospital's patients were low-income, paid by California's Medi-Cal program. The hospital is committed to serve this population but recognizes the need to attract additional price-paying activity or philanthropy to finance this community service mission.

Within a three-mile radius, 14 hospitals share the central Los Angeles market area with CMCLA. Competition is intense.

Recently, a nearby hospital reopened its emergency room in direct competition with California Medical Center Los Angeles. The larger hospitals advertise widely, and compete for the business of the major downtown employers. Within the central city area, all hospitals are suffering a downturn in admissions, patient days and revenues, in reflection of the general recession which is overcoming the hospital industry in California.

Despite this economic picture, a major for-profit hospital chain is planning to build a new 250-bed private hospital in joint venture with the University of Southern California in downtown Los Angeles, beginning in 1986, which will compete directly for the best-insured patients.

OPERATIONS BIAS OF HOSPITAL PLANNING

In the past, long-range planning at California Medical Center Los Angeles had only a two to three-year strategic horizon. Most of the planning effort was focused at the program and service level, driven by operational needs and the annual budget. The hospital had no specialized planning staff, contracting with the corporate planning staff of the parent corporation as needed.

Even without the benefit of a long-range plan, the hospital's Board of Trustees could see the need to replace the main patient care facilities. The Board approved a $35 million building program in 1982, and construction began in 1984. Financing was secured through tax-exempt bonds. The assumptions and provisions in the bond underwriting provided the hospital with a forecast of expected and needed patient volume and revenues to service the debt. De facto, these became the long-range financial plan of the hospital.

At a senior management retreat prior to the decision to move forward with a planning project, it was recognized that California Medical Center Los Angeles needed an innovative approach to rapid changes in its service area and the overall hospital industry.[11] Planning and marketing efforts for hospital programs were fragmented and limited. From the staff assessment, it was clear that marketing expertise needed to be strengthened, and coordinated with planning. The hospital lacked a market research base to quantify its recognition or image among the several key 'publics' it served. Neither the Board nor medical staff were adequately involved in the goal-setting process of the hospital, and there was no overall strategic vision, except in the minds of the CEO and corporate staff, to match the major capital investment to which the hospital was now committed.

NETWORKING: LEARNING FROM THE PRIVATE SECTOR

Through a fortuitous grant from the W K Kellogg Foundation of Battle Creek, Michigan, the hospital became part of a national research and demonstration program called 'Innovations in Health Care Management'. California Medical Center Los Angeles was one of seven hospitals selected from three multi-hospital systems to participate in a research and development project initiated by the Center for Health Management Research (CHMR) of the Lutheran Hospital Society of Southern California.

The working hypothesis of the demonstration project was that innovation in hospital management could be stimulated by 'networking' with the best-managed companies in private industry.[12] Each hospital selected two problem areas for management innovation then sought out innovative solutions from among the top corporations in their community.

With the assistance of Professor George Steiner, a strategic planning expert and member of the advisory board of the 'Innovations' project, the hospital identified and interviewed senior planning staff in a dozen of Los Angeles' most strategically managed companies. These businesses included service industries (Security Pacific National Bank), diversified multi-product companies (Rockwell), and capital-intensive organisations (Southern California Edison).

All industry visits were conducted by the hospital's chief executive officer or by the senior vice-presidents. By conducting the networking activities at the level of top management, CMCLA gained these lessons in strategic management:

commitment to strategic planning and management must come from the top level of the organization;

the 'excellent' companies focus first upon the needs of their customers, then define the lines of business of the corporation;

market-driven strategic plans are organized around products designed for specific market segments; and

product-line management reinforces the link between market-based strategy and operational management planning.

The networking activities triggered a top-level shift in managerial perspective at CMCLA. Senior management was now further persuaded of the value of strategic planning, and set in motion a process both to develop and share the long-range vision of the future across the organization and to create a climate of organizational learning and adaptation.

Becoming a strategically managed organization

With a conviction born from the networking efforts, the senior management group enlisted Board and medical staff in the development of a new strategic mission statement and 20-year goals. Development assistance came from the Futures Program of LHS's Center for Health Management Research. The Futures Program contributed a long-range scan of the health industry for 1985–2000. For each major trend, the strategic implications for California Medical Center Los Angeles were identified. Internally, the capacity of the hospital to respond to the changing environment was assessed.

The process was capped by Board review and adoption of the new mission, a tightly worded statement about the hospital, its values and its desired position in the marketplace. This was flanked by 14 long-range goals which stated the hospital's 20-year directions in areas such as customer commitment, medical staff development, primary lines of business, human resource development, and neighbourhood redevelopment.

Innovative business strategies imbedded in these new goals had been stimulated in the networking exchange with companies whose environments were also experiencing turbulence and competition. Like those companies, California Medical Center Los Angeles determined what its preferred position would be in the market-place. The new directions became the driving forces in the hospital's strategic management:

1 focus lines of business on being a cost-efficient producer of primary health and hospital care;

2 networking with medical staff through joint ventures and 'preferred provider' contracts with major payors;

3 alignment of the hospital neighborhood redevelopment with downtown businesses and the economic redevelopment of central Los Angeles;

4 emphasis on marketing and customer service; and

5 use of the philanthropic fundraising process to extend the hospital's networking and marketing strategies.

ORGANIZATIONAL STRATEGIES: DEVELOPING A STRATEGIC CULTURE

Skeptics of the strategic planning process question the validity of long-range assumptions and the value of making long-term commitments in a continuously changing environment.[13] The critics miss the point. The plan provides a corporate strategic vision whose primary value is symbolic. The new mission statement and goals are not a blueprint, but a corporate philosophy which permeates the managerial culture. All major strategic decisions by California Medical Center Los Angeles are now made consistent with the mission and goals.

For CMCLA, the new mission and goals – four pages in length – became the framework for the continuing process of development of 5-year business plans for major product lines and aspects of hospital development, for example, perinatal services, trauma, an customer relations. In turn, annual department objectives and budgets are set consistent with the 5-year plans.

Within days of adopting the new mission, as chief executive officer (CEO), I initiated a hospital-wide communications effort with key stakeholders inside the organization: medical staff, middle management and employees. They had to buy into the strategic vision, or the plan was simply a piece of paper. It became a process of human resource development, geared to the competitive environment and utilizing an educative, reinforcing leadership model.

The following organizational strategies and incentives were brought to bear to instill an integrated, change-oriented organizational culture at the California Medical Center Los Angeles:

1 establishment of a new marketing department as the primary change agent;

2 joint ventures with the medical staff to increase their bonding with the hospital and their competitive position;

3 transition from a traditional hierarchical structure to decentralized product-line management;

4 management team sharing the vision for strategic decisions, abandoning hard-line advocacy competition for consensus-style decision-making; and

5 creation of new corporate subsidiaries to institutionalize external linkages and provide mechanisms for entrepreneural development.

In pursuing each strategy, the same themes were reinforced: the hospital must change to compete effectively in a competitive environment, and it must continuously learn and be innovative in its products and its management.

ROLE OF THE MEDICAL STAFF

To strengthen the hospital-medical staff alignment, a variety of innovative approaches were developed at the California Medical

Center Los Angeles which recognized the new competitive realities of medical practice. Major medical groups were enlisted to sign up jointly with the hospital in a series of preferred provider agreements with insurance companies, HMOs, and other major payors. The hospital has now entered into 60 such contracts, more than most hospitals. A new 'Independent Practitioner Association' was created by the hospital as a vehicle in which solo physicians and small medical groups could participate in these same contracts with payors. As part of the construction program, the hospital is building a new medical office building with incentives for long-term physician tenancy. The hospital subsidizes a family practice residency program to train young physicians, and to help them build a practice base around the hospital. All these strategies were approved by the hospital's Board and medical staff consistent with the strategic goals, which were referenced often by both groups in the approval process.

These efforts have provided a series of incentives to increase medical staff ownership in the new directions the hospital is taking, and they are working. California Medical Center Los Angeles's admission rate has slipped minimally in 1984, while other downtown Los Angeles hospitals have suffered declines of 6–10 per cent in the past year.

MARKETING AS A CHANGE AGENT

Communicating the strategic vision, inside the hospital and externally, and marketing the new strategies to the hospital's customer bases, are ongoing challenges. At the outset, the hospital needed a global market research base for strategic decision-making. A comprehensive market research survey of nine internal and external publics was conducted in 1984, and will be updated annually. Goals and objectives are being written based on desired changes in the level of recognition of the hospital by its customers, on a product-line basis as well as to assess the overall image of the hospital. The marketing orientation is being extended to all aspects of hospital operations and product development, responding to the challenges of the competitive marketplace.

California Medical Center Los Angeles is gaining an image as a dynamic, future-oriented organization. The new building will provide a dramatic and visible statement of modern medical care. Symbolically, the hospital's entrance has been relocated to face one of the major access routes into the central business district. A hospital-prepared supplement is regularly published in the 'Downtowner' newspaper which showcases hospital development and services. New marketing and advertising campaigns stress CMCLA's role as the community hospital for downtown Los Angeles.

The hospital has used networking and philanthropy to strengthen its relationships with the downtown business community. New Board members have been recruited from top Los Angeles firms, and a new Foundation created to bring more business and civic leadership into the hospital's orbit. The hospital's wholly-owned Redevelopment Corporation is developing a comprehensive land use plan for the 100 acres surrounding the hospital, in cooperation with Transamerica Occidental, a major near-by landholder, and the Los Angeles Community Redevelopment Agency. Enterprising development of housing and commercial buildings is being planned, using a combination of public and private financial sources. Again, networking cements these relationships between the hospital and external organizations.

ADOPTING A STRATEGIC MANAGEMENT STYLE

The networking activities with top companies in the private sector have opened California Medical Center Los Angeles to a new management style suited to the competitive environment. The central principles of the hospital's change-oriented management are:

1 shift in management style from intuitive planning dominated by the CEO to a conscious and participative decision-making by the management team and medical staff;

2 CEO provides leadership by education and communication, not by directives;

3 encourage networking and learning activities of managers and medical staff to develop new partnerships for business development;

4 education and reinforcing incentives for employee development in areas like customer relations and productivity; and

5 managers and medical staff leadership are responsible for strategic planning – there is no separate planning staff.

The new management style is still being adopted and adapted. Product-line management and marketing are now being extended across the range of hospital departments and services. Product-line plans are being written, and new ventures launched. There is a sense of excitement and enthusiasm at the hospital, about a future which no managers are taking for granted.

LESSONS LEARNED

The transition to strategic management has not been without difficulty. Not all of the changes have been welcomed. Recent staff layoffs, the first in a decade, have raised staff anxiety about the future. The hospital was the target of union organizing, which it has successfully resisted. A few managers more comfortable in a highly-structured, predictable organizational environment have departed. Management staff meetings now surface more open conflict than in the past, but the debate is healthy and productive.

Involvement of medical staff centrally in all strategic development activities is clearly one of the critical success factors for the hospital. To gain the support of the medical staff, a Joint Ventures Committee was formed, bringing together the physician leaders with Board members to develop a set of principles about future joint ventures. This statement of corporate philosophy recognized the interests of the medical staff vis-a-vis the hospital, defined mutual responsibilities in joint efforts. Its acceptance by the medical staff and the board has paved the way for cooperation and collaboration.

Conclusion: looking forward

The critical role of the executive in a time of transition is to educate and communicate a sense of the future to the organization. Awareness of the realities of the competitive environment which hospitals face is now broadly shared by medical staff, managers and employees at California Medical Center Los Angeles. They recognize that change is a constant in a shifting marketplace.

Being strategically oriented and market-driven has become the philosophical core of the organization. Networking and organizational learning have opened the windows of the organization to change and fresh ideas, and laid the base for new business relationships.

California Medical Center Los Angeles has a vision of its future, and is not afraid of change. The new attitude is 'think big!' with the same enthusiasm which carried the day in the English comedy, 'The Mouse That Roared'. Hospital staffers are future-oriented. California Medical Center Los Angeles's Nursing Department initiated and is taking a leadership role in redefining the future of nursing in a national study called 'Nursing 2020'. They understand that becoming a strategically managed organization is every manager's responsibility. Even if all the answers are not yet readily apparent, the organization is willing and anxious to learn.

Yet for all the positive strides taken on an institutional level, there emerges from a scanning of recent US trends, a keen awareness that geographically integrated networks of hospitals and other health care services will be the only viable organizations in the near future. The shape of these emerging networks and their ability to successfully adopt and implement a strategic management philosophy remains at issue. Appropriate strategies for reconciling institutional goal-setting with the directions of these 'networks' comprise the new dilemma.

References

1 Ginzberg E. What lies ahead for American physicians: one economist's views. Journal of the Association of American Medicine, 17 May, 1985.
2 Arstein-Kerslake. The downward trend continues. CHA Insight, 8, 10 July, 1984: pp 1–4.
3 Naisbitt J. Megatrends. New York, Warner Books, 1982.
4 Melia E P, Aucoin L M, Duhl L J and Kurokawa P S. Competition in the health-care marketplace: a beginning in California. New England Journal of Medicine, 308, 31 March, 1983: pp 788–792. For follow-up, see also California: a two-year follow-up, New England Journal of Medicine, 311, 13 September, 1984: pp 745–748.
5 Tibbits S J. Competition in California: the new wave from the west. Frontiers of Health Services Management, 4, May, 1985: pp 31–35.
6 Trauner J B. The California health-care market – where is it headed? Frontiers of Health Service Management, 4, May, 1985: pp 4–30.
7 Pattison R V and Katz H M. Investor-owned and not-for-profit hospitals: a comparison based on California data. New England Journal of Hospitals, 309, 11 August, 1983: pp 347–353.
8 Starr, P. The social transformation of American medicine. New York, Basic Books, 1982.
9 A report of the Graduate Medical Education National Advisory Committee (GMENAC) to the Secretary, Department of Health and Human Services. DHHS Pub No (HRA) 81–651, April, 1981.
10 Purdy R J. California physicians: too much of a good thing? California Physician 1, October, 1984: pp 12–15.
11 Parker D. Market driven strategic planning: a case study of California Hospital Medical Center. Foresight, 3, Summer, 1984: pp 6–8.
12 Strum D W and Coile R C Jr. Transferring lessons from high performance organizations. Hospital Forum, 27, May/June, 1984: pp 62–64.
13 Ackoff R L. Creating the corporate future. New York, John Wiley & Sons, 1981.

Developing organisational capabilities

Introduction

By the end of the week-long seminar, there was a recurring recognition in the participants discussions: managers and their organisations must have a capacity for learning. Specialized knowledge and accumulated skills are insufficient to deal with the unique uncertainties, complexities and lack of order which managers confront. Because the phenomena facing the organisation and its managers are always changing, there is no way to prepare in advance a standardised set of techniques that the manager will require to cope with unpredictable problems and opportunities. Instead, there is a need for the manager to be able to continually and rapidly define and redefine what are the important things to which the organisation must attend, and to shape the processes by which they will be managed.

The important role of learning in strategic management had been emphasized in the theme papers by Evans, Parston and Pettigrew. As well as having personal implications for the manager's own development, the inseparability of learning from planning, control and change places an onerous responsibility on the strategic manager to foster and develop organisational learning. This entails a commitment and an ability to analyse and assess performance, and to understand the cause for gaps between intent and outcome. But it also requires an ability to learn when intent may need revision, when current strategies may no longer fit, and when organisational norms and values may have to change.

These recognitions lie at the core of Gordon Best's introductory paper on the sub-theme of development strategy. He argues that the key to building organisational capability and adaptiveness is the development of a capacity in the organisation to engage in effective learning. In this context, the successful strategic manager is constantly concerned with the interplay between the environment and the what and how of managing - that is, the task and process of management. As turbulence heightens, though, the strategic manager must attend principally to process, employing and reflecting upon the continuously changing task agenda to strengthen organisational adaptability and competence.

The paper cites Argyris and Schön's typology of organisational learning: 'single-loop', which is error detection and correction in line with organisational norms; 'double-loop', which connects error detection to the very norms that define effective performance - a sort of double feedback; and 'deutero' or learning how to learn. Best uses these categories to analyse some of the managerial dilemmas that are characteristic of large organisations. These include over-emphases on tasks and on producing results. To overcome these difficulties and to develop the organisation's ability to deliver in changing circumstances, learning to learn must become a key ingredient of strategic management. He concludes the paper by examining how some of the mechanism for accountability and control in the public sector may actually limit the manager's scope for managing strategically, a point that attracted some attention during the seminar debates about the role of public sector managers.

Stephen Leeder's account of the design, establishment and reassessment of a new medical school illustrates how learning to learn can help managers and organisations respond to change. Australia's University of Newcastle Medical School was established to compensate for what its founding fathers saw as an imbalance in traditional medical education. Because of a radically different curriculum and a progressive admissions policy, continuing assessment of performance against expectation is all the more important. However, while students educational performance is good, concerns about how well students will perform in their future work environments is raising some rather disturbing questions about the school's initial objectives and about possible needs for adaptation.

One of the more insightful chapters of this book concludes this section. It is not a prepared paper, but rather the notes of some of the discussions that took place during the Managers as Strategists seminar. In order to initiate discussion about the importance of learning to learn, Gordon Best asked participants to meet first in small groups and to identify and discuss the ways in which they as managers promote learning in their organisations. Each group was asked to consider their own examples of 'single-loop learning' and 'double-loop learning', and then to report back in a plenary session. The notes of two of the small groups discussions are included in chapter 14. While the examples of different types of organisational learning are of some interest, the notes provide a wonderful record of managers reflecting on their own practice, challenging other's ideas, and helping each other to learn.

12

Strategic managing, organisational learning and development strategy

GORDON BEST

What is a strategic manager?

As Tom Evans background paper and some of the other contributions make clear, the concept of managerial strategy has, in recent years, undergone a major reappraisal and reinterpretation. This paper will not attempt to cover this ground again. Yet any contribution to a meeting on the theme of 'managers as strategists' must implicitly or otherwise concern itself with the question of what it means for a manager to behave strategically. In this introduction I will touch briefly upon this issue and then provide an overview of my own contribution to the theme of the seminar.

Over the past 15 years or so, the idea of managerial strategy has attracted considerable attention and been subject to increasing critical scrutiny. As a result, prevailing ideas about the nature of strategy have evolved rapidly in response to a host of insights and 'findings' rooted in both theory and managerial practice. Andrew Pettigrew's recent book[1] provides an authoritative and insightful overview of this evolutionary process. And while it would be an overstatement to say that there now exists a broad consensus as to the nature of managerial strategy, the following three interrelated insights would seem to be the principal products of the process Pettigrew describes.

1 THE 'A PRIORI', LINEAR NATURE OF STRATEGY

Until as recently as a decade ago, the concept of managerial strategy was almost always assumed to incorporate two key subsidiary notions. The first was that a strategy consisted of little more than a preconceived, goal-directed sequence of actions intended to provide a guide for managerial decision-making. The second was the notion that strategy unfolded in a series of overlapping, but essentially sequential phases often described as formulation, implementation, review and appraisal.

In the last decade, however, this 'a priori and linear' view of strategy has given way to a much richer and more complex notion which takes greater account of the *actual* behaviour of senior managers. In essence, this more recent view emphasises the dynamic, evolutionary and yet purposeful nature of strategy as this emerges in the hands of perceptive and proactive senior managers.[2] This perspective portrays senior managers as engaged in a continuous process of responding to the upward flow of information and ideas from within their own organisation and to the challenges and imperatives emerging from the 'external' environment. Strategy, then, both grows out of, and provides a structure for, these two processes. Looked at in this way, it is clear that managerial strategy has no beginning and no end nor does it unfold in a linear fashion: in Quinn's words, '. . . strategies are typically fragmented and evolutionary with a high degree of intuitive content . . . overall strategies tend to emerge as a series of conscious internal decisions [that] blend and interact with changing external events to slowly mutate key managers' broad consensus about what patterns of action make sense for the future'.[3]

2 THE UNITARY NATURE OF STRATEGY

A second key idea about strategy which has been undermined over the past decade is the notion that there is some *one* thing that can be identified as managerial strategy. This notion has been undermined in two ways. The first grows out of the work of writers such as Quinn [4] and Mintzberg[5] who emphasise the *contingent and situational* nature of strategy. Such an orientation recognises explicitly that strategic managerial behaviour is influenced by an ongoing diagnostic process reflecting management's reading of the strengths and weaknesses of the organisation at any point in time. In these circumstances, there can be no one 'correct' idea of strategy but, rather, the recognition that different forms of strategy will be more or less appropriate to differing organisational and environmental circumstances at different points in time.

The second force at work in undermining the unitary view of strategy has been the growing recognition that it is not just 'top management' which has a monopoly on strategic thinking and managing. As Pettigrew has observed: '. . . empirical process research on strategy [has] made a number of descriptive contributions to the understanding of strategic decision-making and change. Strategic processes [are] now accepted as multi-level activities and not just the province of a few, or even a single general manager. Outcomes of decisions are [not] just a product of rational . . . debates, but [are] also shaped by the interests and commitments of individuals and groups, the force of bureaucratic momentum, gross changes in the environment and the manipulation of the structural context. . .'[6]

3 THE INSTRUMENTAL NATURE OF STRATEGY

A third idea central to the early writings on strategy was an emphasis on the instrumental nature of strategy, that is, the notion that strategy was essentially a means for achieving certain ends. From this perspective, two criteria were central to the measure of good strategy: the first was whether the strategy actually enabled management to achieve pre-set ends; the second was whether the strategy enabled management to estimate the consequences of proposed actions before they were taken.

Over the past decade, however, the twin themes of changing organisational context and increasing environmental turbulence have emerged as central in both the literature and empirical work on managerial strategy. As this has happened, it has become increasingly clear that the instrumental view of strategy offers an over-simple and inadequate framework for understanding the process of strategic managing. As a consequence, the instrumental – or means/end – view of strategy has been displaced by a more *developmental* – or process oriented – view. Central to this perspective is the recognition that the environmental and organisational contexts within which managing happens, present challenges and dilemmas which are simply not amenable to definitive analysis. Accordingly, the notions of managerial and organisational learning have emerged as key elements within this developmental perspective. Evans and Best[7] have characterised this perspective as follows: '. . . the 'learning' approach is about process, influence and development. How things are considered and determined is important. [Strategy] must influence *understanding* and action. It is not only how we do things now, but how we invest in their future improvement and development that matters. Because of these factors, the learning model . . . relate[s] the substance of strategy to the developing capacity of the organisation to manage change' (emphasis added).

The picture which emerges from this evolutionary process then, is an altogether more sagacious, complex and above all *relativistic*, view of managerial strategy. And this is perhaps not surprising, for while much of the early work on strategy was based on *a priori* theorising and normative models of strategy, later work was influenced more by descriptive and empirical studies of how managers *actually* manage.

If there is, however, one critical difference which distinguishes the 'old' view from the 'new', it is to be found in the assumed relationship between the *nature of* strategy and the *rationale for* strategy. Within the 'old' framework, this relationship is clear enough: strategy is preconceived and linear; unitary in nature; instrumental and goal-directed; *and therefore* purposeful. Strategic managers behave purposefully *because* they behave strategically. Within the 'new' framework, however, this relationship is more problematic: strategy is non-linear and contingent; situational and pluralistic; opportunistic and developmental; *and yet* purposeful. Strategic managers behave purposefully *in spite of* the fact that they behave strategically. It is this apparent paradox which provides the focus for this paper.

The remainder of this paper is divided into three parts. The next section poses the question, 'How do strategic managers manage?'. In other words, how is it possible for senior managers to develop contingent, opportunistic, developmental forms of strategic managing which also provide direction, coherence and purpose for a large organisation operating in a turbulent environment? The following section examines the processes of managerial and organisational learning which would seem to be central to successful strategic managing and its principal product, development strategy. Finally, the last section poses the question, 'Can public sector managers manage strategically?'. Using the British National Health Service as an illustration, I suggest that the scope which many senior managers have for managing strategically within a public sector environment may be surprisingly limited.

Coming to grips with development strategy: How do strategic managers manage?

This section of the paper explores the process of strategic managing in further depth. For this purpose, I shall make use of the simple diagrammatic model shown in Figure 4. The model is intended to be a schematic representation of some of the principal elements which enter into and influence the process of strategic managing.

The figure suggests that three elements are central to the process of strategic managing. These are: the *tasks* – or whats – of managing; the *processes* – or hows – of managing; and the *environment* – or context – within which managing takes place. Building on this model, I suggest that the effective strategic manager is one who can manage successfully the continuous interplay between task, process and environment so as to deliver changes which are to the advantage of the organisation.

Although Figure 4 is intended to be no more than schematic and suggestive, it is significant that the task and process elements

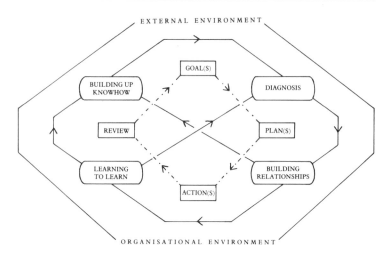

Figure 4 Task process and environment – a simple diagrammatic model
of strategic managing*

are cast as cycles, while the environment is portrayed as con-
textural and ubiquitous. It is worth elaborating further on each of
these three elements.

1 THE TASKS OF STRATEGIC MANAGING

This refers to what Pettigrew[8] calls the content or substance of
strategic change, or what Kotter[9] calls managers' work 'agendas'.
Task refers to *what* it is that managers have to achieve in order to
further the aims of their organisations. Kotter provides a clear description of senior managers' task agendas: 'the agendas . . . managers developed tended to be made up of a set of loosely connected
goals and plans which addressed their long, medium and short-run
responsibilities. As such, agendas typically addressed a broad
range of financial, product/market and organisational issues'.[10]

The four stages in the task *cycle* sown in the Figure are illustrative. Other cycles with more or different stages could be used.
The cycle format is intended to highlight the fact that the achievement of task always requires managers - however informally - to
formulate intentions, plan ahead, decide how to measure achievement, and so on.

2 THE PROCESSES OF STRATEGIC MANAGING

This refers to the ways in which managers go about achieving task
and delivering change. Isenberg[11] distinguishes between organis-

* I am indebted to Robin Coates for introducing me to the task-process cycles.

ational and interpersonal processes by which he means '... the ways in which managers bring people and groups together to handle problems and take action'. Kotter describes how top managers build up 'networks' (of people) and then use these to get action on the items on their agendas. In Kotter's words '... having developed networks that are capable of implementing their agendas, it is not surprising that ... general managers would make sure that they did so'.[12]

The process *cycle* shown in the Figure is again illustrative. It is intended to highlight the fact that the processes involved in strategic managing oblige managers to engage - however informally - in a number of different activities. In casting the process cycle in quite different terms, Quinn[13] points out that: '... [managers] carefully orchestrate ad hoc efforts designed to: ... *sense* developing strategic needs early; *build executive awareness* about options; *broaden support* and comfort levels for action; ...' *build attitudes*, communication channels and resource centres ...', and so on. The arrows passing through the centre of Figure 4 connecting non-sequential phrases of the process cycle are reminders that these processes do not follow neatly one from another but rather, have to be managed in the light of a variety of factors – most notably the states of the organisational and external environments.

3 THE ENVIRONMENT WITHIN WHICH STRATEGIC MANAGING OCCURS

The orthodox view of the managerial environment is that it consists of all those variables which influence the fortunes of the organisation, but which are outside management's control or influence. A more helpful portrayal begins with Pettigrew's useful distinction between the organisational (or inner) environment, and the external (or outer) environment. The importance of this distinction lies in the fact that these two parts of the managerial environment often present quite different problems (and opportunities) for top management.

The environment external to the organisation, for example, consists of such elements as competitors, consumers and the legal system. Changes in the behaviour of any of these groups can – often at quite short notice - pose a major problem or offer an important opportunity for the organisation. In this sense, they can be seen as organisational 'imperatives'; that is, they represent challenges which management must respond to but which, at the same time, management can rarely influence. By contrast, while the inner (organisational) environment can also pose problems and present challenges for management, these can sometimes be influenced directly through managerial action. For example, while the forces of organisational inertia and momentum can often pose quite serious problems for management, they can also sometimes be modified and redirected in order to promote and secure change.

When the three elements described in that Figure are combined, what emerges is a picture of strategic managing which is broadly consistent with the descriptive findings of writers such as Kotter, Mintzberg, Quinn and Isenberg[14]. Thus, it is the selection of tasks or agenda items that top managers attend to over time which – in retrospect at least – sometimes leads to their behaviour being described as *purposeful* and their perspective as *strategic*. Equally, as the environment poses new dilemmas for management, the content of the task agenda and the order in which items are accorded priority, change. It is the ability to see the implications of environmental change for the content and handling of the managerial agenda that is sometimes referred to as managerial *vision* or *foresight*. Finally, as the environmental context and task agenda change, the processes of strategic managing must change also. Sometimes, for example, it will be important to attend to those processes which foster the acceptance of change while, at other times, stabilising and protecting change will take precedence. It is the ability to identify and promote the appropriate processes in changing environmental and task circumstances which sometimes leads us to describe certain managers as *insightful* or *dynamic*.

It is also worth stressing that this complex managing process is not solely driven by changing environmental circumstances or internal organisational momentum. In a dynamic organisation, it will in important part be driven by what we might call managerial *leadership*: that is, the drive to manage the interplay between task, process and environment so as to identify, introduce and then stabilise, changes which are to the advantage of the organisation.

THE NEED FOR LEARNING

It is clear that as organisational complexity and environmental turbulence increase, the difficulties associated with achieving an effective balance between task, process and environment escalate. In particular, surprises in the environment often can bring about abrupt shifts in organisational priorities which, in turn, necessitate changes in the managerial task agenda. Moreover, it should be clear that such surprises, the presence of organisational conflict and other factors which give rise to a changing task agenda, are not infrequent intrusions into managerial practice; they are *central* to management in large organisations. It follows that a continuously changing task agenda is intrinsic to strategic managing.

This observation is the source of the dilemma alluded to in the introduction to this paper: namely, how can the strategic manager manage a changing agenda while, at the same time, maintaining a reasonable level of organisational stability and sense of purpose? Arguably, it is recognition of this dilemma that has led writers such as Argyris and Schön[15], Schön[16], and Michael[17] to adopt a view of strategic managing which emphasises process and, in particular, *managerial and organisational learning*. Indeed, for these writers, the twin concepts of managerial and organisational learning are seen as central features of modern management. As Argyris and Schön have argued:

> Since World War II, some of the most prominent ideas in good currency in American organisations have been those like research and development, organisational innovation, planning and evaluation and the management of change, all of which have to do with (organisational) learning. Awareness of these ideas has passed beyond rhetoric. Most organisations, public and private, now have individual roles and even whole departments whose functions are intended to promote what we would call (organisational) learning. *Managers recognise that they must not only respond to particular changes in the corporate environment, but must also build organisational competence for responding continually to such changes, foreseeable and unforeseeable* (emphasis added).[18]

A central tenet in the writing of these authors is that as organisational complexity and environmental turbulence increase, so too does the need for an emphasis on those processes which facilitate learning. This is because as the task agenda changes, organisational change must follow: but viable organisations – if they are to *develop* rather than simply change – require stability and continuity as well as change. Hence the need for learning as a means of sustaining and informing the process of selective adaption over time.

Writing in a different context, Schön describes this process as follows:

> In general, the more an organisation depends for its survival on innovation and adaptation to a changing environment, the more essential its interest in organisational learning. On the other hand, formal organisations also have a powerful interest in the

stability and predictability of organisational life. .... Surprise, which is essential to learning, is inimical to smooth organisational functioning. Thus organisations evolve systems of error detection and correction whose function is to maintain the constancy of variables critical to organisational life.[19]

Although the process of error detection and correction is only one type of organisational learning, it should be clear in principle that even this elementary form of learning can, on occasion, resolve the apparent conflict between the need for stability and sense of purpose, and the need for continuous change.

Successful strategic managing in a complex and dynamic environment then, requires that the strategic manager attends to process and especially to those aspects of process concerned with learning. At the same time, it is important to stress that successful strategic managing is not solely about change: some learning will reveal the need for stability. Looked at from this perspective, successful strategic managing *is* development strategy.

Managerial and organisational learning: the key to development strategy?

This section of the paper examines in further detail the ideas of managerial and organisational learning as these relate to the process of strategic managing. For this purpose, it is important to try to be as clear as possible about the notion of organisational learning. Argyris and Schön's seminal book, *Organisational Learning: A Theory of Action Perspective*, provides a useful starting point. Argyris and Schön argue that all organisations develop certain norms, strategies and practices which taken together, can be treated as an organisational 'theory of action'. Using this as their starting point, they then turn to the question of what constitutes organisational learning:

> Organizational learning is a metaphor whose spelling out requires us to re-examine the very idea of organization. A collection of individuals organizes when its members develop rules for collective decision delegation and membership. In their rule-governed behaviour, they act for the collectivity in ways that reflect a task system. Just as individual theories of action may be inferred from individual behaviour, so organizational theories of action may be inferred from patterns of organizational action . . .
>
> Organizational learning occurs when members of the organization

act as learning agents for the organization, responding to changes in the internal and external environments of the organization by detecting and correcting errors in organizational theory-in-use, and embedding the results of their enquiry in private images and shared maps of organisation.[20]

In developing this view of organisational learning, Argyris and Schön distinguish between three types of learning which they refer to as single-loop, double-loop and deutero-learning. *Single-loop learning* is simply error detection and correction. It assumes that certain organisational norms exist (for example, for sales or product quality) and that performance may deviate significantly from those norms. When this happens, the reasons for the deviation are sought out, performance modified and the resulting 'know-how' built into the organisation's 'theory of action'. In terms of Figure 4, single-loop learning is a *process* concerned with improving how well *task* is achieved. In Argyris and Schön's words '. . . (single loop learning) is concerned primarily with effectiveness – that is, with how best to achieve existing goals and objectives and how best to keep organisational performance within the range specified by existing norms'.[21]

As noted earlier, however, environmental turbulence and a variety of other factors can often necessitate a major rethink of the task agenda. In this case, *double-loop learning* may be required. Double loop learning consists of questioning and then revising organisational norms themselves:

> . . . [managers] must reflect upon . . . error to the point where they become aware that they cannot correct it by doing better what they already know how to do. They must become aware, for example, that they cannot correct the error by . . . performing öre effectively under existing norms. . .
> We call this sort of double learning *double-loop*. There is in this sort of episode a double feedback loop which connects the detection of error not only to strategies and assumptions for effective performance but to the very norms which define effective performance.[22]

Finally, and perhaps most importantly, *deutero-learning* is defined simply as learning how to learn – that is, an organisation learning how to engage in effective single and double-loop learning:

> When an organization engages in deutero-learning, its members learn . . . about previous contexts for learning. They reflect

on and inquire into previous episodes of organizational learning, or failure to learn. They discover what they did that facilitated or inhibited learning, they invent new strategies for learning, they produce these strategies, and they evaluate and generalize what they have produced. The results become encoded in individual images and maps and are reflected in organizational learning practice[23].

Argyris and Schön, and especially Schön in a later book, stress that senior managers are key agents of organisational learning. The basic assumption is that successful top managers engage in a continuous process of trying to learn how to do their jobs better. Schon describes this process as 'reflection-in-action'.

> Managers reflect-in-action. Sometimes, when reflection is triggered by uncertainty, the manager says, in effect, 'This is puzzling: how can I understand it?' Sometimes, when a sense of opportunity provokes reflection, the manager asks, 'What can I make of this?'And sometimes, when a manager is surprised by the success of his own intuitive knowing, he asks himself, 'What have I really been doing?' ... When a manager reflects-in-action, he draws on this stock of organizational knowledge, adapting it to some present instance. And he also functions as an agent of organizational learning, extending or restructuring, in his present inquiry, the stock of knowledge which will be available for future inquiry.[24]

These observations, which are consistent with the descriptive findings of writers such as Isenberg,[25] suggest that managerial learning is a necessary prerequisite and key input to, organisational learning. In terms of our earlier discussion, these observations suggest that a strategic manager engaged in what we have been calling the learning aspects of process, is contributing to their organisation's capacity to achieve task – *even though* the task agenda may be changing.

COMMON MANAGERIAL PATHOLOGIES

In order to explore how these insights relate to the process of strategic managing and the idea of development strategy, the task-process-environment figure can be used to examine some of the more common managerial 'pathologies' characteristic of large organisations. Consider for example:

1 The *raison d'être* for management resides in the achievement of *task,* while the *effectiveness* of management often depends on

process. In short, managers are not paid to cajole, persuade, build commitment or foster acceptance except as a *means* to achieving certain (task-orientated) ends. On the other hand, managers who cannot do these things well will, on the whole, be ineffective. One important upshot of this is that *while systems of managerial accountability are often task-based, a manager's performance frequently depends on attention to process.* As a consequence, there is often a counter-productive tension betweeen mechanisms of managerial accountability and the strategic time horizon adopted by managers, that is, managers sometimes focus on producing 'visible' short-term results at the expense of developing their organisation's capacity to deliver results over the longer term.

2 A related issue is that too great an emphasis on task can lead to a gap between statements or aspirations of *strategic intent*, that is, statements of *what* change is intended) and the organisation's capacity to actually *implement and deliver* change. Put another way, if the *how* of managing change receives too little strategic emphasis, the organisation's capacity to deliver change will suffer. This is, again, a matter of attending to developmental issues – attending to matters of organisational 'culture'; capability development; shifting attitudes and beliefs; and so on.

3 The converse pathology of placing too great an emphasis on organisational process is also common. In this case, process is dominated by a concern with issues of organisation *inertia* resulting in a change strategy that often amounts to little more than *organisational incrementalism.* Instead of management consisting of the dynamic interplay between task, process and environment guided by a sense of strategic perspective, organisational process is dominant. The consequence is a loss of sensitivity to factors external to the organisation; a task agenda dominated by internal concerns; and a resulting loss of purpose and organisational direction.

All three of these pathologies, in important respects, can be seen to be questions of organisational learning. The first case is perhaps the clearest. Here, the relatively short-term pressures on managers to 'produce results' will result in an emphasis on single-loop learning: that is, on error detection and correction and other forms of learning which are concerned with how best to achieve existing goals. Yet many of the descriptive studies cited by Argyris and Schön and other authors suggest that organisations which are good at this type of learning tend to be rather weak when it comes to double-loop learning: that is, forms of learning concerned with redefining organisational task or mission. There is thus a clear sense in which strategic managers must attend to the development of both forms of learning if they are to successfully manage the tension between the short-term concerns of management accountability, and the longer term requirements of development strategy.

The second and third pathologies are clearly opposite sides of the same coin and, in important respects, raise issues which could be said to be questions of learning how to learn – or deutero-learning. Thus, we have already seen how the management of the task-process interplay is a central feature of managing strategically. In essence, this is about striking an effective balance between task and process given the changing states of the organisational and external environments. In this context, single-loop learning can be seen to be essentially concerned with effectiveness – that is, about how to better achieve task. Double-loop learning, by contrast, can be used to alert management both to the need to engage in different tasks and/or to adopt different processes in order to better achieve task. Clearly, both types of learning are essential if the right balance between task and process – and between short term pressures and longer term developmental needs – is to be struck.

From this perspective then, what Argyris and Schön call deutero-learning can be seen to be a key ingredient of development strategy. It is concerned centrally with *developing* the capacity of the organisation to engage in effective forms of learning. Deutero-learning has little if anything to do with task, it is undiluted *process:* it is concerned with what Tom Evans refers to as building 'organisational capability and adaptiveness' [26]. As such, it is at the very heart of strategic managing and development strategy.

Conclusion: can public sector managers manage strategically?

In this concluding section, I consider some of the implications of the preceding arguments for the management of the British National Health Service (NHS). Before doing so, however, it may be useful to summarise the principal observations put forward in earlier parts of the paper. They are:

The concept of managerial strategy has evolved in recent years to the point where it is now a highly *relative* notion: strategy is seen as non-linear, contingent, situational, pluralistic, developmental and yet purposeful.

When looked at within the task-process-environment framework the process of strategic managing can be seen to exhibit all of these characteristics. The apparent paradox between the nature of strategy and its purposefulness can be restated in terms of the distinction between task and process: that is, while it is task which provides the *raison d'être* for strategy, it is process (which is non-linear, contingent, and so on) which frequently determines how effective strategy is.

As environmental turbulence and organisational complexity and conflict increase, the difficulties associated with managing the interplay between task, process and environment escalate. In particular, as the managerial task agenda changes, management is increasingly obliged to rely on more sophisticated forms of process.

In a complex and dynamic environment, managerial and organisational learning are central to maintaining a workable balance between task, process and environment, as well as that between organisational stability, change and sense of purpose.

When management fails to achieve an effective balance between task, process and environment, a variety of familiar 'pathologies' arise: for example, too great an emphasis on task can result in a gap between strategic intent and operational delivery, while the opposite emphasis can lead to a loss of organisational 'sense of purpose'.

The absence of effective forms of managerial and organisational learning provides one explanation for the existence of such pathologies. The promotion and evolution of effective forms of organisational learning is therefore one of the major challenges facing strategic managers in large organisations; it is also at the heart of development strategy.

MANAGING IN THE NHS

In order to explore what some of the implications of these arguments may be for the management of the National Health Service, we can think in terms of the management of a typical NHS district. Such a district will in many ways be similar to the 'large' organisation sometimes referred to in the strategy literature. It will, for example, have an annual 'turnover' of something like £50,000,000; it will employ around 4,000 staff; and it will cater for something like 250,000 'customers'. It will also display considerable organisational complexity and conflict with, for example, very strong professional groupings pursuing internal strategies which may bear only a passing resemblance to those espoused, and/or pursued, by management. And while, for the most part, management within an NHS district will not face the external challenges of the market place, competitors, and consumers who can buy elsewhere, in recent years, it will have experienced its own special form of environmental turbulence. For example, in the last two years, all NHS district health authorities (DHAs) have had their cash limits altered at least twice and at short notice; they have been instructed to 'privatise' many of their ancillary, domestic and catering services – again, at short notice; they have been instructed to redirect spending from institutional to community services and from acute to non-acute services; they have been instructed to raise 'income' through the sale of NHS properties, to involve clinicians in management, to introduce clinical budgeting, to identify 'efficiency savings' of 1 – 2 per cent per annum, and so on. Not perhaps as dramatic a form of turbulence as some market sector organisations but, nevertheless, clear challenges – and not the only external challenges – to NHS management.

In these circumstances, it seems reasonable to ask whether the observations presented in earlier parts of this paper, might not offer some insights into how the NHS could be managed. In other words, if our descriptions of the process of strategic managing and the nature of development strategy even broadly reflect the realities of managing within large organisations, is their scope for NHS managers to manage strategically?

One reason for posing this question is that a number of the administrative and policy mechanisms which are used or indirectly promoted by central government to 'manage' the service clearly inhibit what senior managers are able to achieve at district (and regional) level. In particular, many of the mechanisms in use for the purposes of fiscal and managerial accountability are largely task-focussed, providing little incentive for district management to attend to process. Consider, for example, three such mechanisms:

1 A hierarchical form of performance review has recently been introduced whereby central government level representatives review the 'performance' of regional health authorities; regional authorities review districts; districts review individual hospitals; and so on. The format and content of the reviews are such that their overwhelming if not sole concern is with *task*. At the level of district review for example, DHA's are asked *what* it is that they have achieved in the past year, and *what* it is they intend

to achieve for the coming year. Process development is largely ignored. It may well be that there is not a single district-level manager within the whole of the NHS that has ever been held to account for the quality of their district's managerial process!

2 Another recent development has been the introduction of NHS 'performance indicators'. These are statistical indices which take various forms and which are intended to allow different health authorities to compare their own 'performance' with that of others. Performance is calibrated in terms of such measures as patient 'throughput'; expenditure per unit of service provided; and so on. DHA's are sometimes ranked nationally on these sorts of indices and the ranks taken into account in performance reviews. And while such comparisons can sometimes be the source of useful insights, there are over 200 such indicators in common use and not *one* relates to what we have been calling managerial process. Managers are not encouraged to think of performance as consisting – even in part – of process.

3 Finally, mention should be made of the NHS planning system. As Tom Evans noted in his background paper, the NHS planning system – although modified and tailored to the perceived requirements of each region – is, in all its forms, still based on a primitive 'forecast and allocate' approach to strategy. That is to say, it is predominately concerned with establishing future targets almost to the exclusion of any consideration of *how* these targets are to be achieved. Put more starkly, although every DHA has a 10-year strategic plan that attempts to set out the principal challenges (tasks) facing the district, *no* DHA has a plan which describes how the district will develop the managerial and organisational capabilities to meet those challenges. Again, process takes a back seat to the preoccupation with task.

Although it would be possible to offer a variety of further examples of such planning and control mechanisms, the point is perhaps clear. Namely, that like many other large public sector organisations, the NHS is rife with bureaucratic and administrative mechanisms *which actually limit the scope managers have to manage strategically and to pursue development strategy.*

As the three examples should make clear, these mechanisms are introduced for accountability purposes and, in particular, to monitor and control the use of resources. And while the need to hold senior public sector managers to account for the use of public resources is real enough, the systems used to do so often *stress task achievement almost to the exclusion of managerial process*[27] Clearly, such a policy is bound in the long term to be counter-productive for it discourages senior management from attending to process, learning and, therefore, development strategy.

Moreover, the prevalent attitude to environmental turbulence (for example, a mid-year reduction in the district's cash limit) and organisational conflict (for example, uncooperative clinicians) is that both simply constitute additional *tasks*. Again, senior management is not encouraged to attend to process (for example, fostering an acceptance of the need for contingency planning); there are no incentives to do so; managers are in no way held to account for not doing so; and if they do so, they are certainly not rewarded. Yet, as we have seen, in situations where environmental surprise and organisational complexity exist, it is *process* that requires strategic emphasis.

It has become fashionable to assert that NHS management needs to be improved and that the evidence for this is that there is a widespread and persistent gap between statements of strategic intent and operational delivery. Management in the NHS – like management in all large and complex organisations – certainly does need to be improved. Perhaps this will happen and the delivery record of management will improve, when NHS managers are encouraged and given the freedom to manage strategically.

References

1 Pettigrew A M. The awakening giant: continuity and change in ICI. Oxford, Basil Blackwell,1985. And see Pettigrew A M. Managing strategic change (chapter 9 of this book, pp 106–127).
2 See, for example, Kotter J P. The general manager. New York, The Free Press, 1982.
3 Quinn J B. Managing strategies incrementally. Omega, International Journal of Management Science, 10,6, 1982.
4 See 3.
5 Mintzberg H. Patterns in strategy formation. Management Science, 24, 9, 1978.
6 See 1: p21.
7 Best G, Evans T. Planning (Appendix I). In: Wickings I (ed) Effective unit management. London, King Edward's Hospital Fund for london, 1983.
8 See 1.
9 See 2: chapter 3.
10 See 2: p 60.
11 Isenberg D J. How senior managers think. Harvard Business Review, Nov-Dec, 1984.
12 See 2: pp 78-79.
13 See 3: p 624.
14 See 2,3,5 and 11.

15 Argyris C. and Schön D A. Organizational learning: a theory of action perspective. Reading, MA, Addison-Wesley, 1978.
16 Schön D A. The reflective practitioner. London, Temple Smith, 1983.
17 Michael D N. On learning to plan and planning to learn. London, Jossey-Bass, 1973.
18 See 15: p 86.
19 See 16: p 323.
20 See 15: pp 25, 29.
21 Ibid: p 21.
22 Ibid: p 22.
23 Ibid: p 27.
24 See 16. pp 241-2
25 See 11.
26 See Evans T. Strategic response to environmental turbulence (chapter 1 of this book, pp 11–31).
27 Smith B L R. and Hague D C. The dilemma of accountability in modern government: independence versus control (especially Chapters 1 and 3). London, Macmillan, 1971.

13

Enviromental assessment in the establishment of a new medical school

STEPHEN R LEEDER

For this paper I have accepted Greg Parston's definition of strategy as the management of the interface between the organisation and the environment.[1] This aspect of management is one of the largest concerns in the development and maintenance of a new community-orientated medical school in Newcastle.

This case study concerns the establishment of that medical school over the past decade. I offer the case in my capacity as a founding member of the school who, for the past five years, has had the chief executive responsibility for the development and implementation of its undergraduate medical education programme.[2,3]

Establishing a new medical school

Newcastle is situated on the Eastern Australian coast, 200 km north of Sydney in the Hunter Health Region of New South Wales. The Hunter is a stable community of nearly 450,000, reflecting the demographic realities of Australia. The region is a major resource for the medical school. The medical school enjoys a close relationship both with the NSW Health Department and private providers of medical care in the Hunter Region. The Hunter Region is comprehensible, stable, large enough and yet small enough to be studied as a community. The Newcastle medical school is more fortunate than others that exist in constantly changing, often volatile and ill-defined, urban settings. As well, the Newcastle community has shown much goodwill and interest in the school and has given clear statements of what it wants from it.

The school was established to correct some of the imbalances in medical education. In the judgement of Newcastle medical school's founding fathers, the broad range of human needs which accompany illness had slipped out of focus. Ironically, medical education had not only lost touch with the human side of medical practice, it had also failed to keep pace with scientific method in its educational approach.

This perception led to two major goals. First, the new medical school is one in which students learn through a patient-orientated, problem-solving approach. It is intended that fundamental medical disciplines, such as anatomy and pathology, should be integrated and learned within the context of medical problems rather than being taught independently of each other and of patient needs. So in the first weeks of the course, students face a problem of a major road crash and so begin their learning about the circulation, respiration, behaviour modification with regard to alcohol use and much else.

The students spend the main part of each week on the university campus in groups, actively mastering what we call 'working problems'. These problems, which reflect the broad range of medical disciplines, are chosen for their commonness, their threat to quality and quantity of life, their treatability and their preventability. This curricular design is, as I will later show, an effort to respond to the contemporary health environment. By this means we seek to avoid the criticism of universities whose irrelevance is captured in the statement that 'whereas communities have problems, universities have departments'.

A second goal is to enhance environmental relevance of our course. We planned to bring students into contact with patients from the beginning of the course. Perhaps as importantly, we also planned contact for them with communities. As part of their early work, students go down coal mines and visit factories and health care institutions. Throughout their first year in the school, the students spend several hours each week in Newcastle localities, ascertaining the profiles of health and illness in these localities, not through the eyes of the medical profession, but by direct contact with community leaders, teachers, clergymen, shoppers and other citizens.

Our first three cohorts of students have graduated, and informal, generally (but not universally) positive, reports attest to the high quality of their early practical performance. A more formal programme of comparative evaluation is in progress.

I wish to use several aspects of the establishment of the medical school to illustrate the interaction of the environment, external and internal, with the process of planning the school and the positive and negative reactions this has generated. The first aspect is the choice of medical students, the second the design of the curriculum, the third the environment of the medical school as perceived by students.

Choosing medical students

Lots of people want to study medicine and, as a result, there is a huge market for medical education. Indeed, the medical student market is so buoyant that the average retailer of medical education relaxes and asks: 'Why bother with complex admission policies when we get the intellectual cream without effort?'. But in skimming the cream of high intellectual achievers for medicine, society has incurred an opportunity cost. Today's genius-level medical students cannot contribute to economics, engineering or the arts.

Another question that should concern admission policies is what sort of doctors will be needed in the 21st century? Today's students will practise medicine in the first two decades of that century. Will the current selection procedures identify those who, by virtue of their aptitude, will make the greatest contribution to the development of the profession, meeting patients' and communities' needs adequately in that future environment?.

In the University of Newcastle we choose medical students in two ways in an effort to respond to these questions and to be experimental. First, we choose on the basis of academic performance either in the high school certificate (HSC) or in a tertiary course. By this means we obtain students from the top one or two centiles of the HSC or equivalent.

Our second admission stream is based on a combination of academic performance and personal characteristics, the latter measured by a battery of psychometric tests supplemented by structured interview with two people, one from the faculty and one from the community. Students admitted via this stream generally come from the top academic decile. Students admitted through either stream may not necessarily have qualifications in science. Mature-age students, aged less than 35 years, are admitted into either of these streams.

STUDENT PERFORMANCE

How have the students done? Is there a discernible difference between those coming in through either door?

Students' overall progress is assessed annually against predetermined criteria. Students are awarded a 'pass' or 'fail', except in the last year, in which ranking has been used to fit graduates into the hospital interplacement scheme. While assessment data are not available by discipline, scores can be calculated for each student comprised of the number and degree of difficulty of items of each assessment which they handled successfully. While we have found a difference between the performance in the first two years of the five-year course of students admitted with or without a science background, the data have shown no difference between the performance of students admitted by either stream. So, in the short-term, students of lesser prior academic achievement do no worse than those of higher achievement. But we have no evidence yet that they do any better, either, although an error of missing a true difference because of small samples cannot be ruled out.

Have we really moved substantially from conventional admission policies, in that all our students come from within the top decile? True, if the contrasts between the two groups were enhanced by choosing stream 2 lower down the HSC table, it would be a more substantial experiment. But in the meantime we cannot support the argument that only genius-level students can do medicine and survive.

Another contentious admission issue relates to minority-group students, in our case Australian Aboriginals. Among several positive reasons for admitting them preferentially, not the least is the impact they may have on the rest of the student body. In 1985 we received Australian federal government support to establish four additional positions for Aboriginal students in each year of our course. Students are eligible from anywhere in Australia. We have no expectations that this manoeuvre will suddenly change the appalling infant mortality rates or adult alcoholism in what is left of the Australian Aboriginal community. But if what has happended among the New Zealand Maoris can be taken as a distant indicator,[4] after two or three generations of Aboriginal doctors, socially conscious Aboriginal medical graduates may concentrate on improving the health of their people.

In 1985, we admitted our first four Aboriginal students. They are surprisingly well qualified. They had not applied to do medicine before because 'no one ever said we could'. Ignorance of what was being offered and lack of self confidence, rather than lack of academic ability, had kept them out. After a year with us they have performed well.

In summary, the medical faculty of the University of Newcastle continues to consider that there are good reasons for critically reviewing admission policies in medical schools in the light of current and projected realities of the environment in which they will practise. Do we consider medicine needs the intellectual cream, and only the cream? Does this yield the best recruits for tomorrow's medical care? To what extent can current admission policies be justified in terms of equity of access for the undisputably underprivileged of which the Australian Aboriginal is a good example? Are these procedures fairer than a lottery? Here are questions of strategy in medical education right at the interface with the environment that call for urgent answers.

Choosing curricular goals and content

The curriculum at Newcastle is a five-year programme which begins with a 10-week introductory term followed by a 27-month course in which problems occurring in all body systems are presented to the student groups. The fourth year deals with the health needs of children and the aged, again presented in problem form. The fourth and final years serve as a junior clerkship. The five-year curriculum is based on learning through the management of clinical problems, in relation to specific behavioural objectives.

Early in the planning of the curriculum, advantage was taken of the community interest in the school by establishing a consultative committee, with community representatives, local medical practitioners, representatives from the NSW Health Department and regional (district) hospitals. The committee commented on and criticised a series of working papers that dealt with all aspects of our development and which have served as central policy statements. Community participation continued after the Consultative Committee was disbanded through the Admissions Policy Committee, on which the citizens of Newcastle have several representatives.

In attempting to design an environmentally responsive curriculum, beside seeking the opinion of community and professional representatives, epidemiologic methods have been applied to the environment to assist in curriculum development. We chose, as the basic building units of the curriculum, roughly 100 problems in contemporary medical practice which the newly qualified doctor may be expected to manage. These 'priority problems' have been chosen on three criteria:

1 A priority problem may be a serious condition, that is, one where appropriate intervention by the doctor may have a decisive effect on the subsequent life expectancy, quality of health, or development of the patient.

2 A priority problem may occur so commonly that the doctor is likely to meet it, or something resembling it, frequently.

3 A priority problem may be one which could have been avoided or minimised by earlier preventative actions.

The resulting list is not exclusively epidemiological, but reflects different and at time conflicting values. Thus, to take 'seriousness', there are a number of conditions, not necessarily common, which are life threatening or potentially disabling, physically, mentally, psychologically or economically, where correct action by a doctor may have a crucial effect on the patient's subsequent life. For example, nobody should die in our society of meningitis (which is uncommon) for lack of a correct diagnosis or treatment with the appropriate antibiotic.

Common problems will form a large proportion of patient contacts in the students' early postgraduate practice. We recognise two dimensions to commonness – the first is epidemiological commonness, the other commonness of presentation in medical practice, the latter reflecting today's pattern of health care. We try to take account of both the epidemiological and health care dimensions of commonness.

For this purpose we have used several sources of data including:

1 The Royal Australian College of General Practitioners' morbidity survey which provides information on the frequency and type of problems presenting for treatment in general practice in Australia.

2 The major causes of death before the age of 65 in Australia from standard published mortality reports.

3 Morbidity survey data produced by the Australian Bureau of Statistics in conjunction with the Health Department of New South Wales for various areas of NSW since 1969.

4 Lists of problems provided by practitioners both within general and specialist practice in the Hunter Region, based upon their own experience, irrespective of specialty.

Many of today's principal causes of mortality, morbidity and economic cost, especially those leading to death before the age 65 (carcinoma of the lung, automobile accidents, and ischaemic heart disease), are potentially preventable. To assist students to acquire skills in effective prevention rather than concentrating exclusively on palliation of existing illness, we present students with a range of problems in which prevention is important.

From a list of about 100 priority problems we have developed a second, longer list. Each priority problem gives rise to a small family of what we term 'working problems'. Thus, chest pain may be a priority problem: derivative working problems would include pleurisy, pulmonary embolism, gastroesophageal reflux and other causes.

The list of 100 priority problems can be modified as faculty, students, health professionals and society change their views on what are the priority problems and as patterns of illness and disease and allocation of tasks among health professionals change. Since the establishment of the first list modifications have been made from time to time in response to concerns about 'omissions' from our original list. In addition, we have not been entirely parochial in defining problems. For example, our priority problem list includes starvation and over-population, problems which have expression in places other than the Hunter Region. The strategy calls for a sensitive appraisal of the external environment to match the education of students to the environmental problems.

Reacting to external and internal environments

> The crucial problems in strategy (are) more often those of execution and continuous adaptation: getting it done, staying flexible[5]

In building a new medical school with community-orientated educational methods, conflict occurred with other medical schools who adhere to traditional educational approaches. Some local medical practitioners did not initially approve of this new educational approach, so different to that experienced in their own medical training. Yet interaction with other medical schools is crucial if our staff are to move as they progress and if the achievements and errors of Newcastle are to have more than purely local (and ephemeral) significance.

While the interaction between the university and local medical fraternity, upon whom we depend for much of our teaching (200 of them, 40 of us), is now generally happy, we have not done well managing the interface with this aspect of our environment. A small investment in personnel management, complicated by the ambiguities of our matrix system, has meant that we have neither trained nor maintained our part-time staff adequately to sustain a strong sense of corporateness between full and part-time staff.

Also, funding for research in Newcastle requires conformity to traditional research grant application formats, publication and attendance at scientific meetings. Grant applications are peer-reviewed by fellow researchers. The conventional Australian approach to research has been so powerful that Newcastle's ideals for programmatic research, directed toward community needs, have struggled to survive. Research at Newcastle is now not greatly different from that occurring elsewhere, except for marginally more emphasis on epidemiological and behavioural topics.

Relations between the medical school and the general community are close and comfortable. The medical school has assisted substantially in securing improved health services in Newcastle and this has enjoyed broadly based community support.

A NEED TO ADAPT

What of the internal environment of the medical school? After a decade of intense effort, many founding Faculty are now jaded and lack the enthusiasm required for prolonged, energising leadership. The environment of learning in which the students live and work received a reflective comment from a management consultant tutoring for the first time in the first year of our course, and it bears restatement. He notes:

> At Newcastle medical school the Maddison (late founding Dean) philosophy and vigor has faded. It does not seem possible, or at least people do not seem to be willing, to lead or to create enthusiasm – perhaps for fear of associating themselves too closely with something which could easily rebound on them as a failure.
> The Maddison approach was to use problem-based learning through doing and participation and to keep students in touch with the real problems and the real communities which they are trained to serve. From the beginning this approach was inconvenient to many ... In this way the vision diminishes ... Once lost, there are all sorts of reasons why non-participating specialists will not inconvenience themselves by once again becoming contributors to the vision and the essential processes involved.

There are many factors that account for his perception, but perhaps none so important as those concerning the relationship academics at Newcastle perceive they have with the traditional world of academia.

Another manifestation of the same problem comes from the other end of the course. A recently-arrived senior lecturer in psychiatry has spent 1985 determining how students perceive their environment. The following report, received recently by the Undergraduate Education Committee, underscores the need to plan strategy carefully with recognition not only of the environment out there but also of the micro-environment one's organisation is creating.

> As part of the recent investigation of the impact of the medical course upon the students, I have interviewed over a third of the student body one-to-one or in small groups within the last few months.

Since the present Year 5 will soon have graduated, I have written the report on them first.

1 The general level of dissatisfaction and distress is high.

2 This level of distress is, though not exclusively, largely course-related.

3 Whilst there are those who feel positively toward their medical training the majority feel at least disappointed, at worst embittered and disillusioned.

4 The principal source of dissatisfaction is levelled at the discrepancy between Faculty ideals and Faculty practice particularly as they converge in the student assessment (examination) process.

5 There is a large subgroup who suffer from psychiatric disorders. In particular the following sources of stress have been noted:

(i) The unpredictability of the assessment (examination) system

(ii) The conflicting messages about what is going to happen at any given assessment.

(iii) That particular assessors are very mood dependent.

(iv) That there is little time for rest, relaxation or leisure.

(v) That there is a chaos of staff and students which despite the best of intentions makes change in the system difficult to sustain.

(vi) That there is little point saying anything about all of the above since the following responses are likely:
   – we've heard it before and know about it and are attempting to do something about it;
   – it reflects a general medical student neurosis;
   – students need to be tough to survive as doctors;
   – it's the same everywhere else.

(vii) That staff are friendly but cannot deliver the promised goods in a reliable, unambiguous way (with a few exceptions).They therefore cannot be trusted.

(viii) That positive feedback is rarely forthcoming, or given grudgingly.

One does not expect euphoria amongst final year students but neither does one expect despair. Many students say that they have changed adversely in their outlook on life. However, the students have not been thoroughly negative. Individual courses, people and Faculty events have been praised. Specific recommendations for change have been made.

After talking with many of the Year 5 students, I have found myself admiring their strength, honesty and humanity. I think it is sad that many will leave believing that it is despite the course we have offered not because of it that they will do well with their medical career.

These comments indicate a major contemporary management problem relating to the environment we have created. The faculty must now adress this question as a matter of great importance.

The institution has reacted strongly and positively to these perceptions. A one-day workshop of all full time Faculty was convened in November 1985 to discuss the report and the problems behind it. Staff members presented suggestions for discussion and debate that included:

1 a student-based mentor scheme whereby older students assume a responsibility for one or more younger students;

2 ways to reduce labour intensive inefficiencies within the education programme, some of which were ideological rather than rational, including the appropriate use of large group demonstrations;

3 ways to improve the coverage of the various disciplines by assessment and greater clarity of responsibility for assessment;

4 a computer-based system to rationalise the complex student timetable;

5 a computer-based information system to assist with personnel management.

The good will manifest by the faculty toward the basic ideals was strong and encouraging. Change may well follow.

Conclusion

It provides an instructive commentary on the power of conservatism to note the relative rarity with which new medical schools adopt policies and programmes which depart significantly from traditional models. An unusual concatenation of circumstances provided the foundation staff at the University of Newcastle, New South Wales, with the opportunity to examine afresh some of the conceptual bases from which medical education has customarily been developed, with particular emphasis on the importance of preparing graduates who would be appropriately equipped to meet the challenges of medical practice in the 21st century. We viewed this as an excellent opportunity to develop a programme which would put preventive medicine into an appropriate context, rather than as an afterthought to a lengthy programme in basic sciences and clinical medicine. It seemed particularly important to try to bridge the tremendous gulf between preventive and clinical medicine which is not only tolerated, but often actively promoted, in the traditional curriculum.

While the intention to create a community-oriented, educationally-modern medical school can be honoured from almost every environmental point of view, the costs are substantial. The energy-expensive process of innovation requires a greater-than-usual investment in personnel management. Micro-environments easily develop which are inimical to the achievement of corporate goals. Vast enthusiasm, physical and emotional strength is demanded of all participants including support staff and students.

References

1 See Parston G. Learning to use plans and guidelines (chapter 5 of this book, p 61).
2 Leeder S R. An Australian approach to medical education: the Newcastle experiment.Medical Journal of Australia, 141, 1974: pp 58–162.
3 Leeder S R. Health for all by the year 2000: educational, empirical and ethical responsibilities for the medical profession. Medical Journal of Australia, 142, 1985: pp 551–555.
4 See Salmond G. 'A New Zealand case study: Maori health' (chapter 2 of this book, pp 32–38).
5 Peters R J. and Waterman T J. In search of excellence. Harper Row, 1982.

14

Notes on organisational learning

The two sets of notes that follow are records of discussions amongst small groups of managers participating in the Managers as Strategist seminar. Each group of participants was asked to identify and discuss the ways in which they as managers promote learning in their organisations.

Group 1: A classification with examples of organisational learning about learning

SINGLE-LOOP LEARNING

1. Time out or retreat. These can be either non-specific, for example, generating values or philosophy or strategy – or specific and task orientated with the outcome unknowable, for example coping with the problem of defining and dealing with the 'do not resuscitate' phenomenon or Exeter local area planning.
2. Learning from mistakes – whether this is a process built into normal management or a specific separately identified 'programme', it is a question of recognising that the important thing about mistakes is not to believe they can be totally eliminated (or suppressed), but to ensure that the appropriate individual organisational learning is secured from the experience.
3. Trend management. Whilst true of all organisations, it is most noticeable in the fashion industry where the name of the game is to spot where the management of an organisation is located on the down slope of the normal curve, whereas we would like to be located on the up curve. The trick therefore is to learn how to spot when the down curve is beginning and then what are actually new trends on the up curve.

DOUBLE-LOOP LEARNING

4. Changing track. Whereby an organisation might well be on course for its declared objective, but changes track towards a new objective which is now deemed to be more appropriate, for example, Len's HMO deciding to market itself on the basis

of quality and expertise stressing the high calibre of their ophthalmologist specialists which resulted in a massive number of new enrolments from elderly people – a bad risk for HMOs and therefore a mistake – so the marketing strategy was switched through some other basis; or Herefordshire Health Authority well on course for changing its mental health services, deciding to use part of an acute psychiatric unit for some other purpose whilst it was still being built.

5. Reorientating to a different context. What may be perfectly reasonable behaviour or a good standard of management becomes no longer good enough in a changed context, for example, Jim's example of a light fingered 'medical' approach to line management to his periphery unit becoming '**** weak', in the context of alleged (but totally unfounded) maltreatment of mentally handicapped children; or Dieter's example of a non-explicit and low profile approach to DNRs no longer being appropriate once this had become a public issue of ethics and professions other than medicine wanted to be part of the action.

6. Unlearning. Meaning learning how to do without what was previously regarded as good attributes, or learning that success does not necessarily depend upon what was previously perceived as predisposing factors towards success, for example, Ron leading his authority away from 'open' relationship with the local media whereby any and all members of the authority might be talking separately to the news media towards a more managerial approach on key strategic or controversial issues; or Jim unlearning a laissez faire medical professional approach to management (which he then characterised as '**** weak') towards a more proactive dynamic management style in the context of the mental handicap on occasions described above; or Bob finding out from the experience of being seconded as district administrator to another district to be just as effective whilst not getting so wound up and high key – 'stay cool'.

7. Evaluation. Meaning evaluation which taught you something about the nature of evaluation and not simply looped feedback on the activity, for example, Jim's evaluation of recidivism in drunken driving cases – this was an extremely imaginative programme which substituted attendance on training programmes for people convicted of drunken driving instead of the usual penal measures which, at the single-loop level, had everything going for them and looked like a very good programme. On proper evaluation it was demonstrated that the programme did nothing to improve the recidivism rate. It has

not only taught the programme sponsors about that particular programme, but also about the nature of most appropriate forms of evaluation.

In addition to these classifications and examples, there were some general points about the critical nature of the top management role in bringing about an organisation with a learning culture. In terms of learning to learn, it is necessary to keep going – one never arrives. This includes having open agendas and even unknowable agendas in advance and including the emotional cost of learning with constant positive reinforcement of the fact of learning. One component of this is the requisite balance between sensitivity and toughness.

Recorder: R W Dearden

Group 2: Learning to learn

I EXAMPLES OF DOUBLE-LOOP LEARNING

A series of examples were proposed by various participants. Jon reiterated his previous example of a reduction in dentists because incidence of dental caries had dropped coupling with a problem that meals supplied to seniors were ending up in the garbage because they could not chew.

Barbara described attempts to implement a standard of providing high security psychiatric beds resulting in a determination that the cost was too great. As such, she proceeded to develop an innovative program focussing on how not to lock up these patients.

Derek described the evolution of his benefits program from one commanding a large market share and thus open to all risks. When government-provided insurance shrank the market, all but the high risk left the program, with a resultant increase in utilization per enrollee. His company made the determination as a result to focus on expanded geriatric services, including moving to retirement villages.

At this point the group began to question these 'war stories' and raised the issue as to whether these were normal management review processes (challenging a standard) versus true examples of double loop learning.

Doug identified the need to be careful and learn from mistakes. He discussed the importance of norms but, even more important, the need to check and rethink norms.

Discussion then focused on the importance of an evaluation

process in place prior to implementing new programs. Formal evaluation was viewed by the group as single-loop learning. It was felt that this process could be pushed toward double-loop learning particularly if fostered within groups. It was noted that there often may be a timing delay in the double-loop learning from such a single-loop process. Ideas may very well occur much later while gardening, sitting in mud baths, and so on.

Andrew then challenged the group as follows: 'Has anyone ever really challenged themselves or their organizations with this issue of learning?'

Rick proposed an example, with which the group concurred, as containing elements of single and double-loop learning as well as learning to learn. At California Medical Center, executive staff recognition of need for a more sophisticated strategic planning effort somewhat serendipitously coincided with the receipt of a grant from the Kellogg Foundation to foster the transfer of innovative management practices from business and industry to the health care sector. As such, executives and senior planners from fifteen major corporations were interviewed by the hospital CEO and senior executive staff. The hospital intent was to purposefuly expose executive staff to different people with different experiences, beliefs and values, while seeking advice as to appropriate modification of the existing planning process. The group agreed that this purposeful exposure with the intent to learn and challenge was an example of the organization learning to learn while the review of the planning process in conjunction with business executives was clearly single-loop learning. Rick reported that as a result of these planning interchanges opportunities were created and pursued in the area of industrial medicine program development, health promotion, philanthropy and others. This opening up of the boundaries of inquiry comprised double loop learning.

Jon proposed the issue of focussing on systems of learning versus learning as a personal and organizational value. He cited an example from his authority wherein the CEO continually acknowledges to the organization that he/she is still learning (value) while implementing personal education of the board (system) and implementing a performance appraisal process with training needs explicitly identified (system).

The group agreed that an iterative process of implementing learning as a value and implementing learning systems was necessary. As such, both could grow together. Elements of the iterative process were identified as follows:

- Leadership accepts the responsibility to set and articulate the value

– Climate setting activities are initiated
– Mechanisms of learning are developed

Concern was raised that development of mechanisms before instilling learning as a value would most probably turn off the process, for example, there was a need to legitimize the process.

II CURRENT CEO RULES

The group agreed that the current focus of their organizations had been single-loop learning and that three had not been much CEO attention to the issue of organizational learning.

Patrick posed the following question: 'When two separate single-loop learning processes converge, do you get double-loop learning?' The group agreed that double loop learning would indeed occur if:

– the group realized it was happening
– there was mutual acceptance
– mutual frame of reference change occurred

It was felt that this seeking of synergy was not so much a process as a mindset or value.

III BLOCKAGES

If CEOs and organizations were not engaged in learning to learn and double-loop learning activities, it seemed appropriate to examine some of the blockages that might be contributing to this behavior. The following examples surfaced:

– rigid adherence to norms and procedures without challenge
– segmentation of the problem-solving process (no boundary crossing)
– contracting perspectives versus expanding perspectives
– lack of an explicit value (learning is important!)
– heavy emphasis on task

It was agreed that innovative organizations had integrated problem-solving processes (boundaries were crossed).

IV MECHANISMS

The group briefly explored various mechanisms to eliminate blockages. Consistent with earlier discussion, it was assumed that the leadership task was complete and that the organization had imbedded learning values. Some mechanisms suggested included:

– introducing ourselves to other beliefs, values and processes
– creating mechanisms to allow people space (brainstorming)
– changing around the cast of characters (cross-fertilizing)
– working down the organization

- formal review and evaluation systems with explicit attention to learning
- structuring of management development processes such that they are multidisciplinary in nature, deal with real issues, and involve people who are directly concerned with those issues.

V SUMMARY

Unable to find many good examples of learning to learn and double-loop learning, the group concluded that there was insufficient CEO involvement in organizational learning to learn and double-loop learning. Consideration of the convergence of single-loop learning processes provided the basis for an examination of blockages to organizational learning and a discussion of mechanisms to facilitate learning.

Recorder: Richard A Norling

Commentary

There are many lessons to be learned from the reflections of these health services managers. When top managers speak openly and critically about their own work, they are trying to articulate what they have already learned from past practice and, by doing so, trying to help improve the way that they themselves – *as well as others* – will work as managers in future. In the course of doing that, happily they disregard the 'mysteriousness of the art of managing', that Donald Schön criticises; they allow us to see how they think, and to think about what they do.

Having had the opportunity during the international seminar of talking with these managers about what they do, and having read many times the papers they wrote, my own learning from their learning has been enlightening and invigorating. The insights are many. A mixture of sensitivity and toughness, leadership in the interplay between task and process, skill to spot the leading edge, a commitment to organisational learning – all of the qualities of the strategic manager that Philip Berman observed – are there. But two insights in particular stand out for me: the first concerns the relationship between the manager and the work of managing, and the second relates to the manager's view of the organisation and its boundaries.

Managers and managing

The work of managing is as multi-faceted as the organisations and problems with which managers deal. In some ways, a theorem of cybernetics seems to apply equally well to management: what is needed to regulate and learn from organisational systems are management systems as variable and complex. Trying to comprehend the variety and complexity of these 'management systems' is no simple task. Tom Evans' strands of strategy and Andrew Pettigrew's triangle of process–content–context are examples of the many conceptual models which are intended to help us understand the dynamics of strategic management. These broad frameworks can aid discussion about the many facets of the work of managers, but – not surprisingly, perhaps – they can be disarmingly simple in portraying the actual interplay of the strategies, processes and tasks that the manager orchestrates.

The manager leads management, particularly in times of crisis. Sometimes the force and clarity of leadership – as Len Schaeffer's role at Group Health demonstrates – may be the heart of the management process. At other times, however, the relationship between manager and managing is less straightforward. George Salmond, for example, is managing a shift in the values and concerns of a national department of health, not least because he seems to think it is the right thing to do. The assessment of environmental issues, the identification of problems and opportunities, and the timing of change are all activities that require his leadership. But in order to manage the needed changes well, he cannot lead them. Instead, he must enable others outside his organisation to do so – those in the Maori community. How does he make the judgements about when to lead and when to enable? Conceptual frameworks of management process don't help answer that question.

Similarly, both Duncan Nichol's and Rick Norling's cases exhibit that obvious, but almost intangible, synergy between the strategic strands of an organisation's development. But what strand precedes what? What development becomes the manager's priority? Will the OD intervention in Wirral Health Authority instill the clear purpose and shared attitudes that are needed to improve performance, or will existing practices first have to be improved – as at California Medical Center – in order to create the fertile ground for building common values and meaningful management development? Once again, conceptual frameworks are silent on this interplay, and that is because what they leave out are the managers themselves. This observation is less facile than it may appear. Although we frequently refer to managers as 'management', we just as frequently disassociate managing from the people who are managers. We treat the work as something which exists separately from the people. But as the managers who have written here show, the two do not exist independently.

It is the manager's judgement that defines the synergy of the management process. It is the manager's diagnosis and commitment to development that interweave the strands of strategy. So, the manager is not merely the manipulator or conductor of some discrete process called management. The strategic manager *generates* the managing process, in which his or her own judgement and values are intrinsic parts. The ways in which the manager reasons and judges and the values which the manager holds are, in a very real sense, the *art* of managing. This integration of the person and the process is demonstrated most clearly in this book by David King's account of how crucial the changes in his own thinking are to the management of change.

Boundaries and control

A second insight that I have gained from these managers' reflections is the importance of their sense of organisational boundaries and of their own abilities to control what goes on within the organisation.

The boundaries of organisations are not always well-defined. They overlap with those of apparently separate organisations. Some organisations, for example, create diseconomies which other organisations are often forced to bear. Dick Knapp's market assessment of the interplay between hospitals and medical education is a good illustration of the point. Even where the composition of an organisation seems clear – as one might assume of a teaching hospital – the actual demarcations can be rather blurry. At the same time, the component parts of organisations are not always in harmony with each other. Sometimes their negotiated orders break down and their shared values and common purposes become challenged: top and bottom don't agree or don't cooperate or simply don't understand each other. In few industries is the negotiated order as complex and as volatile as in health care.

Strategic managers recognise the permeability of their organisations' boundaries and the potential for dissonance within their organisations. But more important than that, they do not manage as if their jobs were simply or always to put things right, to draw boundaries tighter, to get the troops in line. They know it would be foolish to even try. Instead, they form strategies which accept the uncertainties of organisational interplay and which admit, if not foster, the emergence of new and sometimes dissonant ideas from within and from outside their organisations.

Bob Dearden's leadership of the NHS Training Authority's first attempt at strategic planning, for example, was both an exercise to manage the boundary with the Authority's client, the NHS, and an effort to incorporate the many disparate interests of management education within the planning process. By recognising the overlaps and the vested interests, he built the organisation. So, too, Sandy Macpherson's development of a strategy to combat Toronto's AIDS epidemic would not have happened had he not recognised that his public health department's plan was also part of the plans of educational authorities, of voluntary agencies and of community and governmental groups.

These last two examples, in particular, raise the further issue of the differences between public sector and private sector, which occupied so much of the seminar discussion. Clearly, the boundaries of public sector organisations are more than permeable; they are almost imaginary. This must have significant consequences on the ways in which the public sector managers manage and on their strategies. The corollary of what Tom Evans called 'the pooling of risk' in public sector organisations is the pooling of responsibility, the sharing of costs and benefits that is sometimes willfully accepted but always enforced upon the manager. Ineffective education programmes in the NHSTA, for example, will have their ultimate consequences on the efficiency of the National Health Service. At the same time, the NHS may be bearing the costs of poor public housing programmes and, because of geographic rationalisations, imposing costs on public transportation systems. However the budgetary cake is cut amongst public education, health, housing and transportation agencies, the pieces all come out of the same public purse. Unlike the pollution of a private sector manufacturer, the dis-economies of public sector organisations are less easily shifted outside. This financial and political interlocking of public sector organisations has a further consequence on what a manager is being held accountable for: strict organisational performance or broader public sector stewardship. These are issues that need much more reflection, thought and study if we are to understand better what lies at the heart of the public sector/private sector debate in strategic management.

Reflecting on practice

The integration of the person and the process in managing and recognition of the dynamic interface between organisations underscore an important dimension of learning for strategic managers. There is a need for managers to question and assess the influence of *their own* reasoning and judgement on the managing and the performance of the organisation. Coupled to this must be a willingness to alter and adapt their own roles when necessary, as any other part of the management process may need to do. Steve Leeder's paper describes a manager in the middle of this sort of double-loop learning, questioning not only whether his organisation is getting where he wants it to go, but also whether where it is going is still the right place. For a top manager not to ask these types of questions would seem to be either a rejection of learning or a tendency towards despotism. In the end, non-learners fail, and although despots may rule, they do not manage.

There is much more to learn from critical reflections on management, managing and managers as strategists. Happily, as the contributors to this book demonstrate, there are managers who are willing and able to engage in that process.

Greg Parston
September 1986

Managers as Strategists: King's Fund International Seminar, Canberra, Australia, October 1985. List of participants

Barry R Catchlove
Chief Executive
Royal Children's Hospital   *Australia*

R W (Bob) Dearden
Chief Executive
NHS Training Authority   *UK*

Lucy C Dobbin
Executive Director
St Clare's Mercy Hospital, Newfoundland   *Canada*

Jon R Evans
General Manager
North Lincolnshire Health Authority   *UK*

James B Flett
President
Vancouver General Hospital   *Canada*

Pat G Kinder
Chief Administrative Officer
Eastern Health and Social Services Board   *UK*

David King
District General Manager
Exeter Health Authority   *UK*

Richard M Knapp
Director
Department of Teaching Hospitals, Association of American
Medical Colleges   *USA*

Dieter Kuntz
Executive Director
Victoria General Hospital, Manitoba   *Canada*

Bernard J Lachner
President
Evanston Hospital   *USA*

James S Lawson
Assistant Secretary
Department of Health   *Australia*

Stephen R Leeder
Professor of Community Medicine
University of Newcastle   *Australia*
now Professor of Community and Geriatric Medicine,
University of Sydney

Alasdair Liddell
General Manager
Bloomsbury Health Authority   *UK*

A S (Sandy) Macpherson
Medical Officer of Health
Toronto Department of Public Health   *Canada*

John B Mulligan
General Superintendent
Royal Hobart Hospital   *Australia*

Richard A Norling
President and Executive Director
California Medical Center, Los Angeles   *USA*

Duncan K Nichol
General Manager
Mersey Regional Health Authority   *UK*

Ron I Parker
Chief Executive
North Canterbury Hospital Board   *New Zealand*

George Salmond
Deputy Director General
Department of Health   *New Zealand*
now Director General, Department of Health

Leonard Schaeffer
President
Group Health Plan   *USA*
now President, Blue Cross of California

Derek A Shaw
General Manager
Hospital Benefits Association Ltd   *Australia*

J Douglas Snedden
Executive Director
The Hospital for Sick Children   *Canada*

Barbara S Young
District General Manager
Paddington and North Kensington Health Authority   *UK*

Alan Warren
Executive Director
Ottawa-Carleton Regional District Health Council   *Canada*

Faculty

Gordon Best
Fellow
King's Fund College   *UK*
now Director, King's Fund College

Robert Maxwell
Secretary
King Edward's Hospital Fund for London   *UK*

Greg Parston
Fellow
King's Fund College   *UK*

Andrew Pettigrew
Professor of Organisational Behaviour
University of Warwick   *UK*

Sydney Sax
Chairman
National Hospitals and Health Services Commission   *Australia*

Observers

Philip Berman
Director
European Association or Programmes in Health Services
Studies   *Eire*

Thomas Cloher
Director
Centre for continuing Education in Health
Administration   *Australia*

Robert deVries
Kellogg Foundation   *USA*

Errol Pickering
Australian Hospital Federation   *Australia*